JESUS the Refugee

All you need to know about Jesus, his life as a man, and his teachings.

Strong & Bold Publishing
Adelaide, South Australia

JESUS
The Refugee

by

Thai-Nguyen Dang

First electronic edition October 2020

Published by:
Strong & Bold Publishing
a division of Strong & Bold Pty Ltd.
(ABN 59 117 431 384)
Internet: www.strongandbold.com
Email: strongbold@adam.com.au

ISBN 978-0-6487095-3-4

DEDICATION

Dedicated to:

Rev. George Stormont of United Kingdom;

Captain **Jin-An Song (宋謹安)** of Kaohsiung, Taiwan;

UNICEF; and

the City of Duluth, Minnesota, USA.

Foreword by Rex Ward.

Thai is a boat person from Vietnam. In 1978 he embarked on a treacherous voyage in a leaking boat. He eventually was picked up by two Taiwanese fishing boats that rescued him and 28 other people. After some months in a refugee camp in Indonesia, Thai was accepted to go to America.

*I met him in 1968 when he was 13 years old. Besides fighting the Communist as a young Australian soldier in South Vietnam, I also had the duty of teaching English to students of a local high school. Thai was in my class. He did not know me by name but he remembered me as the one who taught him the song "**Five Hundred Miles**".*

*In 2016 Thai came to Australia. Thai tracked me down courtesy of the **Vietnam Veterans Association of Australia** and **1st Australian Civil Affairs Unit Association.** We met, along with his wife Diamond in 2018. It has been 50 years since we last met.*

Thai has a firm faith in God and the work of Jesus. This book captures Thai's dedication to Christ.

Rex Ward, Vietnam Veteran and retired teacher
Avoca Beach, NSW Australia.

Introduction

The purpose of this book is to help the younger generation to understand and accept Christianity. Please note that the word "accept" does not mean following, worshipping or even repenting to Jesus and God. There are a few dozen major Christian denominations in the world at the moment. Each has its own unique style from worshipping to recruiting new members. If you are not a Christian, this book will help you to enter the Christian world with a confident mind-and-heart. The new you and Christian world will have a better chance to live happily together in peace. If you are already a Christian, this book will point out a few facts and lessons that you might have missed while reading your fine-printed thick Holy Bible. These important facts or lessons might not have been brought up in your Sunday school or service either. Regardless of whoever you are, this book is a *narrow door* leading to your happy home.

The core of this book is made up of three chapters. The first two chapters, Chapter One and Two, are derived from the main chapter, Chapter Three. Since the main chapter is very long, reading Chapter One and Two alone will be good enough for the 21st century ever-busy folk. Each chapter contains the collaborated layout that shows and compares the four main books written by Matthew, Mark, Luke, and John. All authors recalled and understood Jesus' teachings or point-of-view differently. Very often more than one author wrote about the same subject. In that case their writings are compiled into a single section.

As for my elaboration part, its pure purpose is to inspire you and me in finding our true faith. It may reflect my ignorance or stupidity but like the questions from a child they all need to be heard.

Overall, you should first focus on Jesus as a man. Whatever you believe or think about him beyond the realm of human being is up to you. I believe that Jesus' earth life alone is worth studying. The least outcome of all is you gain knowledge of Christianity. As Jesus warned his followers two thousand years ago: be aware of the greedy big-mouthed religious leaders and don't follow or worship a fake Jesus.

Well, you must know the real Jesus first before you can spot the phony one!

Thai Dang

References and Credits

1. **Holy Bible**, New International Version NIV, Copyright 2011 by Biblica, Inc. (https://www.biblica.com/bible/)
2. **Life Application Study Bible**, NIV, 2011; published by Hodder & Stoughton in association with Tyndale House Publisher. This book, over 2,000 pages long, has several extra sections that highlight or explain in more detail the verses or chapters. It also has a brief listing or index of 250 major events that happened in Jesus' life.
3. **The Internet:** thousands of websites that were created to serve Christians and non-Christians. This booklet has several details or stories that were posted online but not fully explained in the four Gospels.
4. **Mr. David Plotz** of **www.Slate.com** and his very thorough blog called "**Blogging the Bible**". He pointed out a few good details (and a few bad ones) that could help us understand the Bible better. His blog is like a summary or digest. Here is the link: https://slate.com/news-and-politics/2006/09/the-complete-blogging-the-bible-so-far.html
5. **Microsoft Word:** many clip arts in this booklet are taken from this program. Several grammar guidelines are also very useful for the writer like me whose English is a second language.

Jesus' Brief Biography

Parents: Joseph and Mary of Nazareth
Born: in Bethlehem, around 6 to 5 BC
Died: in Jerusalem, around 30 to 31 AD

Footprints in the Sand

by unknown author.

One night a man had a dream. He dreamed
he was walking along the beach with the LORD.
Across the sky flashed scenes from his life.
For each scene he noticed two sets of
footprints in the sand: one belonging
to him, and the other to the LORD.
When the last scene of his life flashed before him,
he looked back at the footprints in the sand.
He noticed that many times along the path of
his life there was only one set of footprints.
He also noticed that it happened at the very
lowest and saddest times in his life.
This really bothered him and he
questioned the LORD about it:

"LORD, you said that once I decided to follow
you, you'd walk with me all the way.
But I have noticed that during the most
troublesome times in my life,
there is only one set of footprints.
I don't understand why when
I needed you most you would leave me."
The LORD replied:

"My son, my precious child,
I love you and I would never leave you.
During your times of trial and suffering,
when you see only one set of footprints,
it was then that I carried you."

Explanation of Indicators & Symbols

(Mostly applicable to Chapter Three)

- Mark 1:4-5 (to be referred as the **Indicator**) indicating Mark is the author or writer; Chapter 1; Paragraph or Verse 4 to 5. By Googling the Indicator you can access the full version, exactly as written in the Bible.
- Summaries: Following the Indicator there is a summary of the text.
- In the References Section, if the indicators are listed only (no additional writing) then they are duplications. Very often several authors wrote about the same thing.
- **Event Number**: Chapter Three lists all events of Jesus' life-span, either by chronological or event sequence.
- **Event Page** without any adjacent symbol: general details or stories which are useful, but not critical to memorize.
- **Event Page with ↔ Symbol**: details or stories that were not consistently recorded from one writer to the other.
- **Event Page with ↓ Symbol**: too violent, not recommended for readers who are under 17 years old.
- **Event Page with ↕ Symbol**: be advised that the story was either unclear or could not be verified

by other writers. It also appears to be controversial by our modern standards.

- **Event Page with ↑ Symbol**: recommended to be read or memorized since the story has a good impact on our life. If you only have a few minutes to spare, then I would recommend that you focus on these ↑ Events only and to skip everything else.

Brief Background of the Authors

Matthew

Matthew was a disciple of Jesus. Also known as Levi, he was a former tax collector. He published the Gospel of Matthew around 60-65 AD, in Hebrew.

Mark

His full name was John Mark. He was not one of the 12 disciples. This Gospel, believed to be the oldest of the four, was written between 55 to 65 AD.

Luke

Luke was not a disciple of Jesus. He was a Greek doctor, close friend of Paul*. This Gospel was written in 60 AD. Luke was the only Gentile (non-Jewish) author.

John

He was the brother of James (sons of Zebedee). Both were disciples of Jesus. This Gospel was written around 85-90 AD, about 50 years after the death of Jesus.

Note:

**Paul, also known as Saul, was the Jewish authority who originally had ordered to kill and arrest many believers of Jesus (ACT 8:1-3). But at the end, Paul became a very strong believer. He is credited for bringing Christianity to Europe, beginning with Greece and Italy.*

Prologue

If you can only read one page, this is it!

If someone asked me, as a 21st century Bible reader, what would I write in a single line with less than 10 words about Jesus and his teachings? Or what was the most important lesson from Jesus that parents needed to teach their kids?

This would be my answer:

"You cannot serve both God and money."

Matthew 6:24
https://www.biblica.com/bible/niv/matthew/6/

Luke 16:13
https://www.biblica.com/bible/niv/luke/16/

Contents

Chapter One

Seven Interesting Facts You Need To Know about Jesus

There are more facts listed in Chapter Three. You are encouraged to check them all if you have the time.

Fact I

(Event #3 of Chapter Three)

The Birth of Jesus: He was born in Bethlehem to a Jewish family, Joseph and Mary of Nazareth, around 6 to 5 BC* (2025 to 2026 years ago, as of this year, 2020).

References in the Bible

Matthew 1:18-25

Virgin Mary was engaged to Joseph, a carpenter. Before they got married, Mary was found to be pregnant through the Holy Spirit. Joseph was thinking of divorcing her quietly to avoid embarrassment for Mary. However, through his dream, an angel of the Lord appeared and told him to accept Mary as his wife since she was conceived by the Holy Spirit. He was also told to name his unborn son Jesus.

Luke 1:30-34

"How will this be?" Mary asked the angel, "Since I am a virgin."

Elaborations

I just wonder how the authors knew about Joseph's dream. We assume Joseph shared the dream with his relatives or other people. To learn more about Jesus as a human being we should not concentrate on or debate about the belief that Jesus was born to a virgin girl. The aspect of his life and his teaching is more important for us to consider. His contribution to mankind is much bigger than a simple biological issue.

* **Why BC?** In brief, the Romanian-Bulgarian monk named Dionysius Exiguus came up with a calendar in the year 525. He estimated that year 1 was Jesus' birth-year. Later most Christian scholars recalculated Jesus' birth-year based on the New Testament and historical events. They came up with the new timeframe, saying Jesus was born between 4 to 6 years earlier than Dionysius' estimation.

Fact II

(Event #10 of Chapter Three)

Jesus and his parents escaped to Egypt, right after his birth

References in the Bible

Matthew 2:13-15

An angel of the Lord came to Joseph in his dream. "Get up", he said, "take the child and his mother and escape to Egypt. Stay there until I tell you, for Herod is going to search for the child to kill him."

More elaborations

Jesus and his parents were the first refugees in the First Century AD. Just wonder why Christians did not give credit to Egypt for protecting our baby Jesus!

If we stop to think about this event for a minute, then we realize that Jesus' life did not start out peacefully at all. First his mother Mary gave birth to him in a stable (for horses or donkeys) that belonged to someone else. Then right after that his father Joseph dragged both Mary and Jesus across the border, escaping to Egypt. What a tough beginning for the refugee named Jesus!

The world at this moment has more than 80 million refugees who live in leaking tents or cardboard boxes (per **UNHCR**). Like Jesus they left their homeland looking for a safe place. Unfortunately, years after years they are still in the refugee camps.

Fact III

(Event #19 of Chapter Three)

Jesus was baptized by John "the Baptist"

References in the Bible

Matthew 3:13

John the Baptist thought he should be baptized by Jesus instead.

Mark 1:9   Luke 3:21

John 1:31

I myself did not know him (Jesus), but the reason I came baptizing with water was that he might be revealed to Israel.

More elaborations

John the Baptist was a humble man! He was 6 months older than Jesus, his cousin. John knew Jesus would be a blessing for all Jews so he did his best to bring Jesus to the people.

John's main diet was locust and wild honey. Did you know?

Fact IV

(Event #64 of Chapter Three)

The original twelve disciples of Jesus

References in the Bible

Mark 3:13

Peter (aka Simon) and his brother Andrew; James Zepedee and his brother John; Philip and Bartholomew; Thomas and Matthew; James Alphaeus and Thadaeus; Simon the Zealot and Judas Iscariot.

John 1:44

More elaborations

Wonder what happened to Nathanael, one of the first disciples? See John 1:44. Since Nathanael was paired with Philip, some scholars believe **Bartholomew is Nathanael**

Fact V

(Event #46 of Chapter Three)

Jesus' first miracle, turning water to wine*

(*not the first if we count the fish catching "miracle" per John 1:35-51)

References in the Bible

John 2:1-12

When the wine was gone, Jesus' mother said to him, "They have no more wine."

"Woman, why do you involve me?" Jesus replied.

More elaborations

Only John had this story about turning water into wine. Also John was the only one who wrote a little bit about the relationship between Jesus and his mother. Nothing was said about Joseph, Jesus' father.

Fact VI

(Event #207 of Chapter Three)

Jesus' last words, before dying on the cross (being crucified by the Roman soldiers). He was only 35-36 years old.

References in the Bible

Matthew 27:46

*About three in the afternoon Jesus cried out in a loud voice, '**Eli, Eli, lema sabachthani?**' (which means 'My God, my God, why have you forsaken me?)*

Mark 15:33 Luke 23:44-46

"Father, into your hands I commit my spirit."

John 19:30

"It is finished."

More elaborations

Matthew and Mark had the same Jesus' last words. Luke and John wrote something else. That is understandable since none of them was with Jesus at his death. They wrote down according to the accounts and stories of others.

Jesus' last words were not as important as his last image: a very thin, bleeding body hanging on the cross. How agonizing!

Fact VII

(Event #215 of Chapter Three)

After the resurrection (coming back from the death) Jesus first appeared to Mary Magdalene

References in the Bible

Matthew 28:8-10

Suddenly Jesus met them. 'Greetings,' he said. They came to him, clasped his feet and worshipped him.

Mark 16:9-11

She went and told those who had been with him and who were mourning and weeping.

John 20:11-18

More elaborations

Mark and John wrote that Jesus first appeared to Mary Magdalene only. Perhaps that was because she had been very devoted and faithful to Jesus and his ministry. Not like the twelve disciples, one betrayed Jesus and the rest abandoned him when he was in trouble.

Chapter Two

Ten Essential Lessons We Can Learn From Jesus' Teachings

There are more lessons listed in Chapter Three. You are encouraged to learn them all if you have the time.

Lesson One

(Event 27 of Chapter Three)

Jesus' first warning to his disciples and followers

References in the Bible

Matthew 5:11-12

Blessed are you when people insult you, persecute you and falsely say all kinds of evil against you because of me.

More elaborations

Jesus emphasized the challenge of showing your faith. The more you believe in Jesus the more ridicule you will receive from non-believers.

Lesson Two

(Event 29 of Chapter Three)

Jesus' teaching, about light or good deeds

References in the Bible

Matthew 5:14-15

People don't light the lamp and put it under the bowl (hiding it).

Mark 4:21

Do you bring in a lamp and put it under a bowl or a bed? Instead, don't you put it on its stand?

Luke 11: 33-36

Therefore, if your whole body is full of light, and no part of it dark, it will be just as full of light as when a lamp shines its light on you.

More elaborations

Now you understand why your parents put all your cute-looking sketches, awards and diplomas on the walls of their living room. The same you can say about the shelf that is full of your trophies.

As for the light of Jesus, it should not be buried inside a very thick Bible or be hidden inside a massive church surrounded by a high security fence. Jesus' light should be in the open where it could shine on all of us like the sun.

Lesson Three

(Event 36 of Chapter Three)

Jesus teaches about giving to the needy anonymously

References in the Bible

Matthew 6:1-4

So when you give to the needy, do not announce it with trumpets, as the hypocrites do in synagogues and on the street, to be honored by others.

More elaborations

By announcing your generosity you would automatically receive praise and even certificates of appreciations from the public. You can only get the reward once, now or later but not both!

Lesson Four

(Event 39 of Chapter Three)

Jesus advises people about money and wealth

References in the Bible

Matthew 6:19-24

Do not store up for yourselves treasures on earth, where moths and vermin destroy, and where thieves break in and steal.

No one can serve two masters. Either you will hate the one and love the other, or you will be devoted to one and despise the other. You cannot serve both God and money.

Luke 12:20-21

You fool! This very night your life will be demanded from you. Then who will get what you have prepared for yourself?

This is how it will be with whoever stores up things for themselves but is not rich towards God.

Luke 12:33

Sell your possessions and give to the poor. Provide purses for yourselves that will not wear out, a treasure in heaven that will never fail, where no thief comes near and no moth destroys.

Luke 16:13

Lesson Four (continued)

(Event 39 of Chapter Three)

More elaborations

All churches and banks need to have these statements displayed at the door.

Luke had this teaching in two places. Chapter 16 Verse 13 is identical to Matthew's: "You cannot serve both God and Money."

During the Covid-19 crisis, four US Senators were caught selling their stocks in hotel and tourism businesses before the stock market tanked. They were briefed about the virus and knew that would affect their investment. The Americans could have used their effort in stopping the pandemic but instead they decided to serve Money instead of God!

Lesson Five

(Event 40 of Chapter Three)

Jesus teaches about worry

References in the Bible

Matthew 6:25-34

Therefore do not worry about tomorrow, for tomorrow will worry about itself. Each day has enough trouble of its own.

Luke 12:22-26

Who of you by worrying can add a single hour to your life?

More elaborations

This advice is perfect for the Aussie. Despite the expression "*no worries mate*!" people can't help themselves from being worried too much. During the war in Vietnam many young Australians were notified of being drafted to fight (conscripted). While waiting to be sent to the battle field several draftees died because they were overwhelmingly worried or recklessly partied too hard. Only 521 Australians (soldiers and non-armed personnel) were actually killed during the war.

Easy said than done! Worrying is human nature. It is more dangerous than the danger itself. This lesson is very important for all of us.

Lesson Six

(Event 41 of Chapter Three)

Jesus teaches about judging other people

References in the Bible

Matthew 7:1-6

Do not judge, or you too will be judged.

Luke 6:37-42

Why do you look at the speck of sawdust in your brother's eye and pay no attention to the flank in your own eye?

More elaborations

Perhaps God is the one to blame for our shortcoming. Our two eyes can only see outwardly. Judging others is our nature since we don't have the ability to see ourselves.

Also please see Event #123, about a sinful woman who was about to be stoned. I first heard about this "stoning" story through a college roommate. It gave me a very good impression of Jesus. I have started liking him since.

Lesson Seven

(Event 96 of Chapter Three)

Jesus teaches about the words that come out of our mouth

References in the Bible

Matthew 15:18-20

But the things that come out of a person's mouth come from the heart, and these (words) defile them (the speakers).

Mark 7:20-23

More elaborations

Jesus thought a person who spoke with bad words was dirtier than his disciples who did not wash their hand before eating.

The bad habit of not washing their hands is not acceptable, especially now during the pandemic. Shame on the disciples!

Lesson Eight

(Event 113 of Chapter Three)

Jesus tells us to love and treat children kindly

References in the Bible

<u>Matthew 18:10</u>

See that you do not despise one of these little ones. For I tell you that their angels in heaven always see the face of my Father in heaven.

More elaborations

As adults we too have angels guarding us but the angles of children are God's buddies. They have higher authority!

Please do not assume Jesus' word of "despite" means teach or guide. Many times we have seen young children running wild and screaming out loud during the Sunday services in the church. We wish that either their parents or someone from the church could control the bad behavior of those children.

Lesson Nine

(Event 163 of Chapter Three)

Jesus warns against religious leaders who did not appreciate Jesus' youth and his bold teaching style

References in the Bible

Matthew 23:2-3

So you must be careful to do everything they tell you. But do not what they do, for they do not practice what they preach.

Mark 12:38

Luke 20:45-47

They (religious leaders) devour widows' houses and for a show make lengthy prayers. These men will be punished most severely.

More elaborations

It was true back 2,000 years ago. It is still true now. Religious leaders don't do windows! All hard work is done by devoted nuns and followers.

Having a priest sitting at the VIP table in our living room during a party is a big honor. We were trained to look at priests and monks as God, without checking their references. Meanwhile, we do a thorough check of our potential gardener!

Lesson Ten

(Event 220 of Chapter Three)

Jesus' last lesson for his disciple Peter, and us

References in the Bible

John 21:15-18

Very truly I tell you, when you were younger you dressed yourself and went where you wanted; but when you are old you will stretch out your hands, and someone else will dress you and lead you where you do NOT want to go.

More elaborations

That is very true for many leaders, including the Pope. He would rather dress himself casually and walk to a public park or a local pub than perform the duties that the Vatican wanted him to do.

Warning

(To readers who are under 17 years old, and to their parents)

There are several English versions of the Bible out there. Most of them are hard to read or understand. I happened to have an opportunity to read the New International Version (NIV) by Biblica, Released in 2011 and found it more suitable to my reading level. Still, I would not recommend it to any reader who is under 17 years old. I picked the age of 17 since in the USA movie theatres do not allow anyone under 17 to watch X-Rated movies. The sexual and violent acts in the Bible, especially the Old Testament, are too much for most youngsters. Of course, I used the term "most" since I have not seen all the latest video games nowadays. When the arcade video game named Mortal Kombat came out about 25 years ago I thought it was very violent...

Even if you are over 17, the Bible is still very troublesome not to mention very dark and the logic of its writers is difficult to grasp. Unless you want to become a priest, a pastor, nun, or an expert in Christianity, reading the current Bible page by page is likely a waste of time. Even if you have plenty of time to waste, you still can't remember it all. So why not leave the complete Bible reading project to the experts? With your smart phone you can access any quote or story in the Bible just by using a few simple motions of your fingertips.

For all Christians, the most relevant aspect of the New Testament Bible is the story of Jesus. Four authors who wrote about Jesus are Matthew, Mark, Luke, and John. Only Matthew and John were Jesus' original disciples (students or devoted followers). I assume they had taken notes or heard stories from other believers during the short life of Jesus. Comparing their four main books or Gospels you will see that some details are not consistent from one writer to the other. Furthermore, one author might have covered things that Jesus did while others left out completely. We could understand that because these books were written at different times by four different writers who were not closely interfaced. Also, their writing was reconstructed according to Jesus' speaking, not Jesus' writing. Therefore the sentences are choppy, lengthy, and very hard to follow or understand. Furthermore, both Mark and Luke were not with Jesus during his teaching period. Therefore, whatever they put down was not from hearing Jesus directly, but rather from the other people, including the 12 disciples of Jesus.

Finally, please use your own judgment to weed out fiction from fact. A belief is only good if it does not harm you and your family, either mentally or physically. With a good heart-and-mind you can avoid the traps that were set up by the profit-driven organizations. Twice Jesus cleared out many vendors who turned the temple into a marketplace (see **Event 153**).

Unfortunately, many churches and temples are now operating just like the time of Jesus. The merchandise may be changed from doves, donkeys, and cattle to beautiful statues of Jesus or property investment opportunities. Still, someone will need to clear out the money-making businesses in God's house. Since Jesus is not with us at the moment someone will have to take his place. So hopefully for the third time the one who will do the clearing is YOU!

Chapter Three

Life and Death of Jesus, according to Matthew, Mark, Luke, and John

This compiled guide was created to help readers of all faiths understand Jesus, his brief life and painful death.

Event 1

John the Baptist, son of

Zechariah (a priest) and his wife, Elizabeth

References in the Bible

Luke 1:5-25

Do not be afraid, Zechariah; your prayer has been heard. Your wife Elizabeth will bear you a son, and you are to call him John.

The angel said to him, "I am Gabriel. I stand in the presence of God, and I have been sent to speak to you and tell you this good news."

More elaborations

John the Baptist was 6 months older than Jesus. They were cousins. He was a very important part of Jesus' life. See Event 19 about the baptism of Jesus.

Event 2

Nazareth is the hometown of Jesus' parents

References in the Bible

<u>Luke 1:26-37</u>

God sent an angel Gabriel to Nazareth, a town in Galilee, to a virgin pledged to be married to a man named Joseph, a descendent of David.

More elaborations

Gabriel is the same angel who came to see Zechariah and Elizabeth (parents of John the Baptist).

It must be a shock for Mary. She was a poor, young woman without high expectation. Being engaged to Joseph was a big step of her life but that was nothing comparing to being the mother of the Messiah. She was overwhelmed with responsibility and the ridicule of her peers. Joseph, her fiancé came close to leaving her. Worst of all, her son would be rejected and murdered.

↑Event 3

The Conception of Jesus: he was born in Bethlehem to a Jewish family, Joseph and Mary of Nazareth, around 6/5 BC (2025 to 2026 years ago, as of this current year, 2020).

References in the Bible

Matthew 1:18-25

Virgin Mary was engaged to Joseph, a carpenter. Before they got married, Mary was found to be pregnant through the Holy Spirit. Joseph was thinking of divorcing her quietly to avoid embarrassment for Mary. However, through his dream, an angel of the Lord appeared and told him to accept Mary as his wife since she was conceived by the Holy Spirit. He was also told to name his unborn son Jesus.

Luke 1:30-34

"How will this be?" Mary asked the angel, "since I am a virgin."

More elaborations

I just wonder how the authors knew about Joseph's dream. We assume Joseph shared the dream with his relatives or other people.

To learn more about Jesus as a human being we should not concentrate on or debate about the belief that Jesus was born to Mary, a virgin girl. Once you read the rest of this book you will see that the virgin-mother issue is not relevant in helping us find our faith.

Event 4

Mary visits Elizabeth and stays at her house for three months

References in the Bible

<u>Luke 1:39-56</u>

But why am I so favored, that the mother of my Lord should come to me? As soon as the sound of your greeting reached my ears, the baby in my womb leaped for joy.

More elaborations

Both Elizabeth and Mary were pregnant at the same time. Although Elizabeth was living at a higher standard for being richer, she felt the honor of being visited by Mary, the mother of our Lord.

Event 5
John the Baptist is born

References in the Bible
Luke 1:57-80
When it was time for Elizabeth to have her baby, she gave birth to a son.

John 1:6
There was a man sent from God whose name was John.

More elaborations
"No! He is to be called John." In naming the child, Elizabeth had more power than her husband!

The birth of John the Baptist is a miracle by itself. His mother, Elizabeth already passed her child-bearing age. She and her husband, Zechariah, felt shameful of being childless. In the Jewish culture back then that was considered as a punishment from God.

Event 6
Jesus was born in Bethlehem

References in the Bible

Luke 2:1-7

So Joseph also went up from the town of Nazareth in Galilee to Judea, to Bethlehem the town of David, because he belonged to the house and line of David. He went there to register with Mary, who was pledged to be married to him and was expecting a child. While they were there, the time came for the baby to be born, and she gave birth to her firstborn, a son. She wrapped him in cloths and placed him in a manger, because there was no guest room available for them.

More elaborations

The term "manger" made people believe that Jesus was born in a stable (built for horses and donkeys). The Jews expected him, a Messiah, to be born in a big royal palace and to a wealthy family.

Event 7
Shepherds visit Jesus

References in the Bible

Luke 2:8-19

So they hurried off and found Mary and Joseph, and the baby, who was lying in the manger.

More elaborations

Why did the angels announce the birth of Jesus to the ordinary shepherds? Was there a connection? Perhaps by doing that God confirmed that even the humble and the poor were still God's children. If there is good news for mankind then why not let them know too.

Event 8
The three wise-men (Magi) visit Jesus

References in the Bible

Matthew 2:1-12

After Jesus was born in Bethlehem in Judea, during the time of King Herod, Magi from the east came to Jerusalem and asked, "Where is the one who has been born king of the Jews? We saw his star when it rose and have come to worship him."

More elaborations

The Magi or wise-men from East of Jerusalem saw the rising star and came to look for Jesus. They announced that the newborn Jesus was "King of the Jews". That did not go well with the Jews in Jerusalem and King Herod.

Big mouthed Magi revealed too much about Jesus! King Herod would not know if they kept their visit as a low profile. These "Wise-men" were not really wise!

↓ Event 9

King Herod wanted to kill Jesus

References in the Bible

Matthew 2:13-16

When King Herod heard the news about the "new King of the Jews" born in Bethlehem he was furious. Since the Magi did not tell him the whereabouts of the new born Jesus King Herod issued an order to kill all babies who were two years old or younger.

More elaborations

Also because of the Magi's big mouth, innocent babies were killed by King Herod!

This is a good lesson for all of us to learn. Before we tell someone important news about something we have to stop and think. The birth of Jesus was a great joy for mankind but to King Herod it was a big threat to his own kingdom. He felt he had no choice but to try killing the baby Jesus!

↑ Event 10

Jesus and his parents escaped to Egypt

References in the Bible

Matthew 2:13-15

An angel of the Lord came to Joseph in his dream and told him to take Jesus out of Israel and go to Egypt. He was asked to stay there until further notice.

More elaborations

Jesus and his parents were the first refugees in the First Century AD. I wonder why Christians did not give credit to Egypt for protecting our baby Jesus.

If we stop to think thought about this event for a minute then we realize that Jesus' life did not start out peacefully at all. First, his mother Mary gave birth to him in a stable (for horses or donkeys) that belonged to someone else. Then right after his birth, Jesus' father Joseph dragged both Mary and Jesus across the border, escaping to Egypt. What a tough and humble beginning for the first refugee named Jesus!

The world at this moment has more than 80 million refugees who live in leaking tents or cardboard boxes (per **UNHCR**). Like Jesus they left their homeland looking for a safe place. Unfortunately, years after years they are still in the refugee camps.

↕ Event 11
Mary and Joseph bring baby Jesus to the temple

References in the Bible

Luke 2:21-24

"On the eighth day, when it was time to circumcise the child, he was named Jesus, the name the angel had given him before he was conceived."

More elaborations

Luke appears to have wrongly written this verse. The newborn Jesus and his parents had already left for Egypt, to escape King Herod the Great.

Event 12
Jesus returned to Nazareth

References in the Bible

Matthew 2:23

After the death of King Herod an angel appeared in Joseph's dream and told him to take his family back to Israel.

More elaborations

Another dream of Joseph was mentioned. Perhaps in the old days people lived a simpler life. Their minds therefore were easily connected to the spiritual world. Getting a message from an angel in our dreams is common like we receive a text message from friends.

↑Event 13
12-year old Jesus speaks to the religious teachers

References in the Bible

Luke 2:41-52

After three days they (Mary and Joseph) found him in the temple courts, sitting among the teachers, listening to them and asking them questions.

More elaborations

It took them three days to find the young boy Jesus? He was the first "Home Alone" boy character.

Jesus was luckier than Joseph (son of Jacob). He could be kidnapped and sold to slave owner. At 17, Joseph was sold by his own brothers to the Ishmaelite merchants who then took him to Egypt. The course of Jewish state was changed for the better because of this unfortunate event. If you want to find a good, inspiring story of all in the Old Testament then this is the one:

Genesis 37:26-28.

↔ Event 14

Introduction to the Gospel of John (the disciple of Jesus)

References in the Bible

John 1:18

No one has ever seen God, but the one and only son, who is himself God and is in the closest relationship with the Father, has made him known.

More elaborations

In his book, John the disciple of Jesus clearly stated that "no one has ever seen God." Even Moses, the closest one to God was not even allowed to see God.

However that statement does not fit the story in the Old Testament. The book **Genesis** section 5 paragraph 1 (Genesis 5:1) told us that a human being was created with the likeness of God. Furthermore in Genesis 32:22-30, Jacob (descendant of Adam and Eve) not only met, but even had a wrestling match with God, ***and won***! God blessed Jacob and changed his name to Israel. Jacob and his Israelite clan were the founders of the great nation later named Israel.

↑ Event 15
John the Baptist: the creator of Baptism and Confession

References in the Bible

Mark 1:4-5

The whole Judean countryside and all the people of Jerusalem went out to him (John the Baptist). Confessing their sins, they were baptized by him in the River Jordan.

John 1:23

I am the one of calling in the wilderness, "Make straight the way for the Lord."

More elaborations

John the Baptist was the first trailblazer, preparing the path for Jesus!

Not sure if there was a book or gospel written separately for John the Baptist. He had started a ministry before Jesus began teaching. The growth of Christianity should at least be 20% credited to John the Baptist and his teaching.

↔ Event 16

John the Baptist predicts the coming of Jesus

References in the Bible

Matthew 3: 11

I baptize you with water for repentance. But after me comes one who is more powerful than I, whose sandals I am not worthy to carry.

Mark 1:7

After me comes the one more powerful than I, the straps of his sandals I am not worthy to stoop down and untie.

John 1:26

More elaborations

What is right, "to carry" according to Matthew or "to stoop down and untie" according to Mark and John?

As we will see later on, both John the Baptist and Jesus gave up their life for their strong belief. Both died young, in their early 30s.

Event 17

John the Baptist prepares the way for Jesus

References in the Bible

Matthew 3:1-3

In those days John the Baptist came, preaching in the wilderness of Judea and saying, "Repent, for the Kingdom of heaven has come near."

Mark 1:1-8

Luke 3:1-17

John 1:29

More elaborations

John the Baptist set out to do what he had to do: besides laying a path for Jesus' ministry he also provided the credit (like job references) to a younger Jesus.

↑ Event 18
John the Baptist was living and preaching in the wilderness of Judea

References in the Bible

Matthew 3:4-6

John's clothes were made of camel's hair, and he has a leather belt round his waist. His food was locusts and wild honey. People went out to him from Jerusalem and all Judea and the whole region of Jordan. Confessing their sins, they were baptized by him in the River Jordan.

Mark 1:6

More elaborations

Not sure how the locusts were cooked. There was no oil for deep frying so I assume he grilled them. Andrew Zimmerman is not the first person to eat "Bizarre Food".

This should be a lesson for many priests and monks. To achieve your true faith or even enlightenment you should put yourself in a remote nature place where you can concentrate on your mission of serving God. Big cities or busy metropolitan areas are for the people who want to serve Money.

↑ Event 19
Jesus was baptized by John the Baptist

References in the Bible
Matthew 3:13
John the Baptist thought he should be baptized by Jesus instead.

Mark 1:9

Luke 3:21

John 1:31
I myself did not know him (Jesus), but the reason I came baptizing with water was that he might be revealed to Israel.

More elaborations
John the Baptist was a humble man. He was 6 months older than Jesus, his cousin. John knew Jesus would be a blessing for all Jews so he did his best to introduce Jesus to the people.

John's main diet was locust and wild honey. Did you know that?

Event 20
Jesus was tempted by Satan

References in the Bible

Matthew 4:1-11

After the baptism Jesus was led by the Holly Spirit into the wilderness. For 40 days and nights Jesus was tempted by Satan.

Mark 1:12

More elaborations

Either Satan did not have any power over Jesus or Satan did not do a good job of studying Jesus before putting out the bait.

Is Satan a man or woman? I think neither since man or woman is a classification for humans only.

Event 21
Jesus begins teaching in Galilee

References in the Bible
Matthew 4:17
Repent, for the kingdom of heaven has come near.

Mark 1:14-15

Luke 4:16

John 4:43-45
A prophet has no honor in his own country.

More elaborations
Both Jesus and John the Baptist had the same message for the Jews: "Repent. Become a follower of Christ or risk losing a chance of getting into heaven."

Galilee was Jesus' hometown but people there did not repent to him. "*Bụt Nhà Không Thiêng*", a Vietnamese phrase that means "Buddha is not sacred in his own house". You will read later that even Jesus' own brothers did not even believe in him.

↔ Event 22

Jesus provides a miraculous catch of fish

References in the Bible

Luke 5:1-7

Master, we've worked all night and haven't caught anything. But because you say so, I (Peter) will let down the net.

More elaborations

Per John 1:35-51, Peter was introduced to Jesus by his brother Andrew. However, author Luke wrote that Jesus met Peter/Simon while he was fishing. Not sure who is right!

Event 23
Jesus' first four disciples

References in the Bible

Matthew 4:18-22

The first four disciples were all fishermen. The first pair was Simon also known as Peter, and his brother Andrew. The other pair was James and his brother John. Both were the sons of Zebedee.

Mark 1:16

John 1:35-51

More elaborations

The first disciple Andrew had actually already followed John the Baptist. But he jumped to Jesus' bandwagon when he heard high remarks about Jesus from his former teacher, John the Baptist.

Event 24

Jesus teaches with authority in Capernaum*

References in the Bible

Mark 1: 22

The people were amazed at his teaching, because he taught them as one who had authority, not as the teachers of the law.

Luke 4:31-36

More elaborations

What did Jesus teach? Luke mentioned that Jesus' words had authority. We can only assume that Jesus' teaching resonated with his audience.

***Where is Capernaum?** Capernaum is a fishing village on the northern edge of Sea of Galilee. It is actually a fresh water lake, largest one in Israel. Capernaum was the place where Jesus met several of his disciples. He also established his ministry there.

Event 25
Jesus drives out the impure spirit in a man

References in the Bible

Mark 1:23-25

"Come out of him!" The impure spirit shook the man violently and came out of him with a shriek.

Luke 4:33-36

More elaborations

Is this a miracle? Both Mark and Luke wrote about this event that happened in a synagogue.

We all have seen that many priests did the same to the demon-possessed followers in their Sunday services. Perhaps there are a couple of priests in the world who have the same power as Jesus, but I doubt that all of them do.

↔ Event 26

Jesus gives the 8 beatitudes (blessings)

References in the Bible

Matthew 5:1-10

Blessed are the poor in spirit, for theirs is the kingdom of heaven.

Luke 6:17-26

Blessed are you who are poor, for yours is the kingdom of God.

More elaborations

Jesus only said one way but Matthew and Luke wrote down two different ways.

"Poor in spirit" is not the same as "you who are poor".

Why 8 blessings? These eight beatitudes very much covered everything regarding to our life and faith back in Jesus' days, like Ten Commandments that God gave us through Moses. If Jesus come back to us tomorrow very sure he will add a few dozen more beatitudes like "*Bless those who are bullied online, for theirs is the glory in Facebook.*"

Event 27
Jesus' first warning to his disciples and followers

References in the Bible

Matthew 5:11-12

Blessed are you when people insult you, persecute you and falsely say all kinds of evil against you because of me.

More elaborations

Jesus emphasized the challenge of showing our faith. The more you believe in Jesus, the more ridicule you will hear from the non-believers.

↑ Event 28

Jesus teaches about salt

References in the Bible

Matthew 5:13

Salt is good only when it still has its saltiness.

Mark 9:50

(Mark also wrote about salt here)

Luke 14:34-35

More elaborations

During the time of Jesus, salt was rare and valuable. He used salt as a metaphor for our good character.

↑ Event 29
Jesus teaches about light or good deeds

References in the Bible
<u>Matthew 5:14-15</u>
People don't light the lamp and put it under the bowl (hiding it).

<u>Mark 4:21</u>
Do you bring in a lamp and put it under a bowl or a bed? Instead, don't you put it on its stand?

<u>Luke 11: 33-36</u>
Therefore, if your whole body is full of light, and no part of it dark, it will be just as full of light as when a lamp shines its light on you.

More elaborations
Now you understand why your parents put all your cute looking sketches, awards and diplomas on the walls of their living room. The same you can say about the shelf that is full of your trophies.

As for the light of Jesus, it should not be buried inside a very thick Bible or be hidden inside a massive church surrounded by a high fence. Jesus' light must be in the open where it can shine on all of us like the sun.

Event 30

Jesus teaches about the law

References in the Bible

Matthew 5:17

Do not think that I have come to abolish the Law or the Prophets. I have not come to abolish them but to fulfill them.

More elaborations

Not abolish the law? The Jews were hoping for a new Kingdom where they could have wild parties 24/7. How disappointing!

↑ Event 31
Jesus teaches about anger

References in the Bible
Matthew 5:22
But I tell you that anyone who is angry with a brother or sister will be subject to judgment.

More elaborations
If we could forgive strangers who sinned against us then why would we not forgive our loved ones?

Jesus actually mentioned "murder" and "anger" in the same teaching session. Both are considered as terrible sins because they violate God's command to love.

Event 32
Jesus teaches about lust

References in the Bible
Matthew 5:28
But I tell you that anyone who looks at a woman lustfully has already committed adultery with her in his heart.

More elaborations
I assume this applies to a woman who looks at other men lustfully also has committed adultery in her heart.

Jesus emphasized that if the *act* is wrong then so is the *intention*. I guess we have to eliminate our fantasies and avoid any place that allows "*looking but no touching*".

↕ Event 33

Jesus teaches about divorce for the first time

References in the Bible

Matthew 5:31-32

But I tell you that anyone who divorces his wife, except for sexual immorality, makes her the victim of adultery.

Luke 16:18

Anyone who divorces his wife and marries another woman commits adultery, and the man who marries a divorced woman commits adultery.

More elaborations

In the early times, society and Jesus put the burden on men regarding to the action of divorce.

This part of guidance is not well received in this day and age. A wife is not the property of a husband. Marrying a divorced woman is not a sin!

↑ Event 34

Jesus teaches about revenge

References in the Bible

Matthew 5:38-42

And if anyone who wants to sue you and take your shirt, hand over your coat as well.

More elaborations

A challenge for all of us: to forgive and be kind to the ones who hurt us. This teaching is similar to Buddha's: "*Từ Bi Hỷ Xả*".

As the world becomes more populated, the traffic in big cities proves to be a challenge for everyone. How do you keep yourself calm while other drivers do all kinds of things that bother you? The term of "road rage" was not around during Jesus' time, but it is very common now to hear that term mentioned on TV almost every day. In serious cases, several people died as a result.

What happened to our good, friendly nature? We have stopped caring or considering for anyone else but ourselves. I guess that is a sad outcome of the rat race where we are the contestants.

Just forgive the violators and concentrate on your journey. Life on the road is tough but getting to the destination is even tougher. Be cool and be safe!

Event 35
Jesus teaches about loving the enemy

References in the Bible

Matthew 5:43-47

But I tell you, love your enemies and pray for those who persecute you, that you may be children of your father in heaven.

Luke 6:27-36

More elaborations

Perhaps this is one of the most difficult lessons to learn or practice. But being true children of God, you and I have to show our love to everyone, even enemies. Perhaps they deserve to be loved more than others, including our "loved ones".

↑ Event 36

Jesus teaches about giving to the needy anonymously

References in the Bible

<u>Matthew 6:1-4</u>

So when you give to the needy, do not announce it with trumpets, as the hypocrites do in synagogues and on the street, to be honored by others.

More elaborations

By announcing your generosity you would automatically receive praise and even certificates of appreciation from the public. You can only get the reward once, now or later but not both!

Event 37
Jesus teaches about prayer

References in the Bible

Matthew 6:5-8

Do not be like them (who prays out loud), for your Father knows what you need before you ask him.

More elaborations

God also can understand any languages that you are thinking in your head. English is optional!

↑ Event 38
Jesus teaches about fasting

References in the Bible

Matthew 6:16-18

When you fast, do not look somber as the hypocrites do, for they disfigure their faces to show others they are fasting.

More elaborations

Good virtue but hard to follow! Seeking attention and admiration from others is our natural behavior. A few of us managed to hide our pain or our "sacrifices" for a while but then publish our high achievement later on through tell-all books or TV documentaries.

↑ Event 39
Jesus teaches about money and wealth

References in the Bible

Matthew 6:19-24

Do not store up for yourselves treasures on earth, where moths and vermin destroy, and where thieves break in and steal.

No one can serve two masters. Either you will hate the one and love the other, or you will be devoted to one and despise the other. You cannot serve both God and money.

Luke 12:20-21

You fool! This very night your life will be demanded from you. Then who will get what you have prepared for yourself?

This is how it will be with whoever stores up things for themselves but is not rich towards God.

Luke 12:33

Sell your possessions and give to the poor. Provide purses for yourselves that will not wear out, a treasure in heaven that will never fail, where no thief comes near and no moth destroys.

Luke 16:13

↑ Event 39 (continued)

More elaborations
All churches and banks need to have these statements displaced at the door.

Luke had this teaching in two places. Chapter 16 Verse 13 is identical to Matthew's: *"You cannot serve both God and Money."*

During the Covid-19 crisis, four US Senators were caught selling their stocks in hotel and tourism businesses before the stock market tanked. They were briefed about the virus and knew that would affect their investment. The Americans could have used their effort in stopping the pandemic but instead they decided to serve Money instead of God!

Believe in the Power of Prayers

↑ Event 40
Jesus teaches about worry

References in the Bible
Matthew 6:25-34
Therefore do not worry about tomorrow, for tomorrow will worry about itself. Each day has enough trouble of its own.

Luke 12:22-26
Who of you by worrying can add a single hour to your life?

More elaborations
This advice is perfect for the Aussie. Despite the expression "*no worries mate*!" people can't help themselves from being worried too much. During the war in Vietnam many young Australians were notified of being drafted to fight (conscripted). While waiting to be sent to the battle field several draftees died because they were overwhelmingly worried or recklessly partied too hard. Only 521 Australians (soldiers and non-armed personnel) were actually killed during the war.

Easy said than done! Worrying is human nature. It is more dangerous than the danger itself. This lesson is very important for all of us.

↑ Event 41
Jesus teaches about judging other people

References in the Bible
<u>Matthew 7:1-6</u>
Do not judge, or you too will be judged.

<u>Luke 6:37-42</u>
Why do you look at the speck of sawdust in your brother's eye and pay no attention to the flank in your own eye?

More elaborations
Perhaps God is the one to blame for our shortcoming. Our two eyes can only see outwardly. Judging others is our nature since we don't have the ability to see ourselves.

Also please see Event #123, about a sinful woman who was about to be stoned. I first heard about this "stoning" story through a college roommate. It gave me a very good impression of Jesus. I started liking him since that time.

↕ Event 42
Jesus teaches about asking, seeking and knocking

References in the Bible

Matthew 7:7-12

Ask and it will be given to you; seek and you will find; knock and the door will be opened to you.

Luke 11:5-13

I tell you, even though he will not get up and give you the bread because of friendship, yet because of your shameless audacity he will surely get up and give you as much as you need.

More elaborations

Interesting lesson about reputation! The man helped you because he cared about his reputation or because he hated to be bothered at night, not because of his friendship with you.

Anyway, keep knocking until you get what you wanted but be careful. People react differently especially when they were bothered late at night. If you are in Texas USA then please be ready to dodge the bullets.

↑ Event 43

Jesus teaches about the way to Heaven or The Kingdom

References in the Bible

Matthew 7:13-14

Enter through the narrow gate. For wide is the gate and broad is the road that leads to destruction, and many enter through it.

Luke: 13:22-24

Make every effort to enter through the narrow door, because many, I tell you, will try to enter and will not be able to.

More elaborations

The metaphor of a narrow door: all good places are hard to get in. Most prestigious schools or universities are just like that.

Congratulations to any readers who recognized the phrase *"narrow door"* was used in my introduction to this book!

Event 44

Jesus uses fruit as a metaphor for people's actions or their children

References in the Bible

Matthew 7:15-23

A good tree cannot bear bad fruit, and a bad tree cannot bear good fruits.

Luke 6:43-45

A good man brings good things out of the good stored up in his heart, and an evil man brings evil things out of evil stored up in his heart. For the mouth speaks what the heart is full of.

More elaborations

"*Nhìn Quả Biết Cây*", Vietnamese phrase means from looking at the fruit we can figure out its tree.

There are a few exceptions: durian and dragon fruit. Durian tree is beautiful but its fruits are ugly and stinky. Dragon fruit tree (more like a vine) looks ugly and scary but produces beautiful and tasty fruits.

Event 45
Jesus teaches about building on a solid foundation

References in the Bible
Matthew 7:24-27
Therefore anyone who hears these words of mine and puts them in practice is like a wise man who built his house on the rock.

Luke 6:46-49

More elaborations
Easier said than done! Jesus' words are not just simple words but rather a life-long lesson. Putting good words in used is hard since we tend to follow a quick and easy path, like cutting corners. If the good words are considered as the instruction manual then we would skip reading it and start assembling the IKEA table right away.

By the time we finished putting all pieces together we just then realized that the table did not look right. The drawer was put in a wrong location and we still had many extra pieces.

↑ Event 46

Jesus' first* miracle, turning water to wine

(*not the first if we count the fish catching "miracle" per John 1:35-51)

References in the Bible

John 2:1-12

When the wine was gone, Jesus' mother said to him, "They have no more wine."

"Woman, why do you involve me?" Jesus replied.

More elaborations

Only John had this story about turning water into wine. Also John was the only one who wrote a little bit about the relationship between Jesus and his mother. Nothing was said about Joseph, Jesus' father.

↑ Event 47
Jesus clears the temple full of livestock for sale

References in the Bible

John 2:13-16

In the temple court he saw people selling cattle, sheep and dove, and others sitting at tables exchanging money.

"Get these out of here! Stop turning my Father's house into a market!"

More elaborations

Well, at least back then the church goers did get something back from the money that they brought with them to the church. Nowadays after the Sunday church service, your wallet is empty and you have nothing to show for it!

Event 48
Jesus' second miracle, to heal a man with leprosy

References in the Bible

Matthew 8:1-4

A man with leprosy came and knelt before him (Jesus) and said, "Lord, if you are willing, you can make me clean.'"

Mark 1:40

Luke 5:12-16

More elaborations

Touching a leprosy man without gloves is a no-no since it is very contagious. But Jesus accepted the risk because he wanted to heal the poor leper with faith.

Not sure why Jesus did not want the people who were healed to spread the good news? More than once Jesus told the people who were healed by him "not to tell anyone else".

Event 49

Jesus' third miracle, to heal a servant of the Roman Centurion

References in the Bible

Matthew 8:5-13

Lord, I do not deserve to have you come under my roof. But just say the word and my servant will be healed.

Luke 7:1-10

More elaborations

The first case of tele-healing, how impressive! Today we sometimes can get the diagnosis and treatment through virtual or internet doctors. But still, we must take the medicine for the illness. So, keep Jesus in mind when the doctors are not available or when they already gave up on you.

The Roman Centurion was like an Army officer. He was the conqueror. Reaching to Jesus, a Jew, for help was an act of desperation and faith.

Event 50
Jesus' fourth miracle, to heal Peter's mother-in-law

References in the Bible
Matthew 8:14-15
He touched her hand and the fever left her, and she got up and began to wait on him (Jesus).

Mark 1:29

Luke 4:38

More elaborations
Bad use of the miracle! Jesus should have made her well and sent her to a nice place to rest, not to hang around and wait on him like a maid.

Event 51

Nicodemus (a Pharisee) visits Jesus secretly at night

References in the Bible

John 3:1-21

Jesus replied, "Very truly I tell you, no one can see the kingdom of God unless they are born again."

More elaborations

Nicodemus was expecting Jesus to point him to an easy path to the Kingdom of God. Like Paul, Nicodemus turned out to be a great believer.

↕ Event 52
Disciples John and James have bad tempers

References in the Bible

Luke 9:51-56

Lord, do you want us to call fire from heaven to destroy them?

More elaborations

Talk about impatient and the abuse of power. John and James were the first century gangsters!

James and John are brothers. James was always mentioned before John so we can assume he is the older one. James is known for his temper and selfishness. To his credit, he was the first disciple to be killed for his faith.

Event 53
John the Baptist glorifies Jesus

References in the Bible

John 3:22-30

He (Jesus) must become greater; I must become less.

More elaborations

John the Baptist did his job well by introducing Jesus to the Jews. He was an ascetic prophet known in Christianity as the forerunner of Jesus. Still, he was very modest and humble; always try his best to glorify Jesus.

John preached about God's Final Judgment and baptized repentant followers in preparation for it. Jesus was among the recipients of his rite of **baptism**.

↑ Event 54
Jesus teaches about the cost of following him

References in the Bible

Matthew 8:20

Foxes have dens and birds have nests, but the Son of Man has nowhere to lay his head.

Luke 9:56-62

John 16:1-4

They will put you out of the synagogue.

More elaborations

Jesus did not want his disciples and followers to expect much from him. In fact he knew most of them thought about the Kingdom of God as a large government with a big palace and budget. Each of the disciples would have a high position in Jesus' cabinet.

Event 55

Jesus heals many people

References in the Bible

Mark 1:33-34

The whole town gathered at the door, and Jesus healed many who had various diseases.

More elaborations

What? Healing everyone without asking them for the Health Insurance or Medicare card? No wonder Jesus didn't own expensive Gucci shoes or a big Mercedes!

Event 56

Jesus talks to a Samaritan woman at the well

References in the Bible

John 4:1-30

Everyone who drinks this water will be thirsty again, but whoever drinks the water I give them will never thirst.

More elaborations

Jesus broke the rules by speaking to the Samaritan woman. As it turned out, that first contact had led to the success of spreading Christianity among non-Jews.

What rule was that and why? For centuries there were conflicts between Jews and Samaritans. Although both groups are descendants of the same ancestors but they drifted apart due to the difference in religious and political beliefs. Jesus, a Jewish man, talking to a Samaritan woman, was not considered appropriate.

Event 57

Jesus does all the hard work for us

References in the Bible

John 4:34-38

I sent you to reap what you have not worked for. Others have done the hard work, and you have reaped the benefits of their labor.

More elaborations

It does not happen all the time, but now and then we get a good break! Of course we must appreciate others who have done the hard work for us.

Event 58

Jesus heals the son of a government official

(without seeing or touching the sick son)

References in the Bible

John 4:46-54

Then the father realized this was exact time at which Jesus had said to him, "Your son will live." So he and his whole family believed.

More elaborations

This is the second tele-healing miracle (only John had this story). See Event 49 when Jesus healed the servant of a Roman Centurion.

Event 59

Jesus heals a lame man by the pool

References in the Bible

John 5:1-15

When Jesus saw him lying there and learned that he has been in this condition for a long time, he asked him, "Do you want to get well?"

More elaborations

Jesus had to ask, if the man wanted to get well since some people preferred to be disabled for a reason like not wanting to work!

↔ Event 60
Jesus sends demons into a herd of pigs

References in the Bible

Matthew 8:28-34

When he (Jesus) arrived at the other side in the region of the Gadarenes, two demon-possessed men coming from the tomb met him. They were so violent that no one could pass that way.

Mark 5:1-20

He gave them (demons) permission, and the impure spirits came out and went into the pigs. The herd, about two thousand in number, rushed down the steep bank into the lake and were drowned.

Luke 8:26-39

More elaborations

Another inconsistent story here: Matthew mentioned "two demon possessed men" while Mark and Luke wrote just "a demon possessed man."

Well, even if it was just one man Jesus demonstrated his power over the demon. In our time, we are facing the demons every day in our lives. They are in various forms, such as drug dealers and child molesters. Without Jesus being here with us, you and I have to use our strong faith in God to fight these 21st century demons.

Event 61
Jesus heals a paralyzed man

References in the Bible
Matthew 9:1-8
Take heart, son, your sins are forgiven.

So Jesus said to the paralyzed man, "Get up, take your mat and go home." Then the man got up and went home.

Mark 2:3-12

More elaborations
Before Jesus could heal the man, he had to forgive the man' sins first since they were the root cause of his illness. However, teachers of the law and religious leaders thought Jesus was blaspheming. They believed that only God could forgive our sins.

↑ Event 62
Jesus eats with sinners

References in the Bible
Matthew 9:9-13
It is not the healthy who need a doctor, but those who are ill.

Mark 5:15

Luke 5:27-32

More elaborations
As a tax collector, Matthew' skill helped Jesus to manage his entourage and ministry. As for eating, most sinners actually had money to pay for the food. Therefore, hanging around with them was a good idea!

Matthew also became a good writer who put together a complete story of Jesus known as The Gospel of Matthew.

Event 63
Jesus answers about fasting

References in the Bible

Matthew 9:14-17

Then John's disciples (the Baptist) came and asked him (Jesus), "How is it that we and the Pharisees fast often, but your disciples do not fast?"

Mark 2:18-19

Luke 5:27-32

More elaborations

Mark said "some people" but Matthew mentioned that the people who asked Jesus about fasting were the disciples of John the Baptist.

↑ Event 64
Jesus chooses 12 disciples

References in the Bible

Mark 3:13

Peter (aka Simon) and his brother Andrew; James Zebedee and his brother John; Philip and Bartholomew; Thomas and Matthew; James Alphaeus and Thadaeus; Simon the Zealot and Judas Iscariot.

John 1:44

More elaborations

Wonder what happened to Nathanael, one of the first disciples? See John 1:44. Since Nathanael was paired with Philip, some scholars believe **Bartholomew was Nathanael.**

Event 65
Jesus unknowingly heals a bleeding woman

References in the Bible

Matthew 9:20-21

"If I can only touch his cloak, I will be healed." Jesus turned and saw her. "Take heart daughter, your faith has healed you." And the woman was healed at that moment.

Mark 5:21-34

More elaborations

She had been sick for so long she could not wait any longer. She was so desperate and wanted to treat herself. She was a typical "go-getter", an active or self-serve patient.

Event 66
Jesus revives the dead son of a widow

References in the Bible

Luke 7:11-17

He (Jesus) said, "Young man, I say to you, get up!" The dead man sat up and began to talk, and Jesus gave him back to his mother.

More elaborations

Only Luke had this story. The poor woman, she had already lost her husband and now her only son. Jesus felt her sadness so he decided to perform his most powerful miracle of all: bring the dead back to life.

Event 67

Women accompany Jesus and his disciples

References in the Bible

Luke 8:1-3

Mary (called Magdalene) from whom seven demons had come out, Joanna the wife of Chuza, the manager of Herod's household; Susanna; and many others. These women were helping to support them (Jesus' group) out of their own means.

More elaborations

Besides playing the supporting roles to Jesus and his disciples, these women were also the sponsors or financiers of Jesus' ministry: **Food before Faith!**

Event 68

Jesus revives a dead girl

References in the Bible

<u>Matthew 9:18 & 23</u>

After the crowd had been put outside, he (Jesus) went in and took the girl by the hand, and she got up.

<u>Mark 5:35-43</u>

<u>Luke 8:40-56</u>

More elaborations

Same deal per Jesus, "Don't tell anyone that I just healed you." I could only assume that Jesus had a limited amount of blessing as part of his earth-bound mission. Jesus wanted to use his power for well-deserved people, not just everyone.

The other reason is Jesus only has a limited amount of time on earth. He rather wants to use his precious time to teach his disciples about healing others instead.

Event 69

Jesus heals two blind men

References in the Bible

Matthew 9:27-31

Then he touched their eyes and said, "According to your faith let it be done to you", then their sight was restored.

More elaborations

Not just one but two blind men were healed by Jesus at once. However Jesus emphasized that they were healed because of their deep faith in Jesus.

Event 70
Jesus makes the mute speak

References in the Bible

Matthew 9:32-33

And when the demon was driven out, the man who had been mute spoke.

More elaborations

In the same room, right after Jesus had healed the two blind men he then used his power to drive out the demon and cured the mute man, allowing him to speak. Jesus was really busy, I would say.

Event 71

Jesus sent out the 12 disciples, in pairs

References in the Bible

Matthew 10:1-15

Do not go among the Gentiles or enter any town of the Samaritans.

Mark 6:7

More elaborations

It sounded like a racist order but Jesus preferred to recruit the Jews only at the beginning. This turned out to be a mistake. Most Christians in the world today are not Jewish.

↔ Event 72

Jesus sends out 72 messengers

(not just 12 disciples)

References in the Bible

Luke 10:1-16

Go! I am sending you out like lambs among wolves. Do not take a purse or bag or sandal; and do not greet anyone on the road.

More elaborations

Only Luke wrote about this story, sending 72 messengers. I assume they were split into several teams. Otherwise it would be hard for anyone to host or care for them. The Hilton was not built back then.

↔ Event 73
The 72 messengers return

References in the Bible
Luke 10:17-24
Blessed are the eyes that see what you see. For I tell you that many prophets and kings wanted to see what you see but did not see it, and to hear what you hear but did not hear it.

More elaborations
Again, only Luke added this story about 72 messengers. Matthew noted that Jesus only sent out 12 disciples in pairs which made more sense. Jesus' homeland was still very small. An entourage of 72 people plus supporters would be overkill.

Event 74

Jesus prepares the disciples, to have a game plan

References in the Bible

<u>Matthew 10:16-42</u>

I am sending you out like sheep among wolves. Therefore be shrewd as snakes and as innocent as doves.

More elaborations

That's a tall order! You can't be both: snake and dove. Although in our daily life, you cannot stick to just one character. Too nice? Someone will take advantages of you!

Event 75

Jesus eases John the Baptist's doubt

References in the Bible

Matthew 11:1-16

Are you the one to come, or should we expect someone else?

Luke 7:18-23

Blessed is anyone who does not stumble on account of me.

More elaborations

Very tough question from John the Baptist! He had put all his faith, and hope in Jesus in saving the Jews. He did not want to be wrong with his own disciples and followers.

↑ Event 76
Jesus promises rest for the soul

References in the Bible
Matthew 11:28
Come to me, all of you who are weary and burdened, and I will give you rest.

More elaborations
Jesus offered to trade his light-loaded yoke to our heavy-burdened yoke. How nice!

Do you know anyone who wants to take the heavy load and leave the light one for you? People tend to do the opposite, trying to get by with minimum work. After their shopping trip to the supermarket most would abandon their shopping cart (trolley) anywhere in the parking lot. Bringing it back to the store or to a designated area seems to be a very hard job. They can't even carry their own light load. How do you expect them to carry the heavy load for you?

Event 77

A sinful woman washes Jesus' feet

References in the Bible

Luke 7:36-48

You (Peter Simon) did not give me a kiss, but this woman, from the time I entered, has not stopped kissing my feet. You did not put oil on my head, but she has poured perfume on my feet. Therefore I tell you, her many sins have been forgiven.

More elaborations

Only Luke has this story. Not sure how Peter felt when Jesus compared the sinful woman to him.

↔ Event 78

Jesus’ disciples eat wheat (or corn) on Sabbath

References in the Bible

Matthew 12:1-2

At that time Jesus went through the grain-fields on the Sabbath. His disciples were hungry and began to pick some heads of grain and ate them.

Mark 2:23

Luke 6:1-5

More elaborations

Without permission from the farmer, picking wheat (or corn) was an act of stealing.

The Hodder & Stoughton Publisher (UK) uses the term “ears of corn” instead. That is wrong since corn was only grown in North America, mainly Mexico. Columbus began bringing it back to Europe after his discovery of America in 1492.

Event 79

Jesus heals a man's hand on the Sabbath

References in the Bible

Matthew 12:13

Then he (Jesus) said to the man, 'Stretch out your hand'. So he stretched it out and it was completely restored, as sound as the other.

Mark 3:1-5   Luke 6:6-11

More elaborations

Jesus got into trouble for healing a sick person on the Sabbath. Still, the inflexibility of the religious belief in not doing anything on the Sabbath really annoyed Jesus. People who were hurt or sick should not have to wait until Monday.

Event 80
Jesus heals a demon-possessed blind and mute man

References in the Bible

Matthew 12:22

Then they brought him a demon-possessed man who was blind and mute, and Jesus healed him.

More elaborations

Jesus had healed two blind men and a mute man before, but not a man with both issues at once. A new challenge, but nothing Jesus could not handle.

Event 81

Jesus argued with religious leaders who accused Jesus of using Satan to fight off Satan

References in the Bible

Matthew 12:24-28

If Satan drives out Satan, he is divided against himself. How then can his kingdom stand?

Mark 3:23-30   Luke 11:17-20

More elaborations

The establishment and religious leaders did not like a newcomer with too many talents and power. Jesus was a threat to them therefore they tried everything to eliminate him.

↑ Event 82

Jesus teaches about our spoken words

References in the Bible

Matthew 12:37

For by your words you will be acquitted, and by your words you will be condemned.

More elaborations

Jesus talked about Judgment Day when we all would be judged. What comes in through our mouth may make us sick and what comes out of our mouth may get us into trouble.

Event 83
Jesus played down the role of his earthling relatives, including his mother

References in the Bible

Matthew 12:48-49

"Who is my mother and who are my brothers?" Pointing to his disciples, he said, "here are my mother and my brothers."

Mark 3:31

Luke 8: 19-21

More elaborations

Poor Mary! She loved him no matter what.
No one said anything about Joseph, Jesus' father!

"Anh Em Xa Không Bằng Láng Giềng Gần". That Vietnamese phrase means "brothers/sisters who live far away are not important as the neighbors who live next door."

↑ Event 84
Jesus gives lesson about planting seeds, a metaphor for his teaching

References in the Bible

Matthew 13:1-8

Still other seeds fell on good soil, where it produced a crop.

Mark 4:2-8

More elaborations

Jesus' teaching is like the seeds. Only a few of us could understand and flourish.

"*Nước Dổ Lá Môn*", a Vietnamese proverb means pouring water over the taro leaf does not make it wet. The lesson, no matter how good it is, can only be learned by the students who are willing to learn.

Event 85

Jesus explained to his disciples about using parables

References in the Bible

Matthew 13:11

Because the knowledge of the secrets of the kingdom of heaven has been given to you, but not to them (the general public).

More elaborations

Not everyone is well educated or smart. Jesus had to reach his audience by using the folksy style, simple expression or things to which the mass population could relate to.

Event 86
Jesus' hometown (Nazareth) did not believe in him

References in the Bible
Matthew 13:53-58
A prophet is not without honor except in his own town and in his own home.

Mark 6:1-6   Luke 4:24   John 4:44

More elaborations
"Bụt Nhà Không Thiêng", a Vietnamese phrase means "Buddha is not sacred in his own house." We tend to look outward to fancy imports and ignore our own domestic products. Both Buddhism and Christianity were more welcomed by the outside world as "imports".

Event 87
The arrest of John the Baptist

References in the Bible

Matthew 14:3-4

Now Herod had arrested John (the Baptist) and bound him and put him in prison because of Herodias, his brother Phillip's wife.

Luke 3:19

More elaborations

John the Baptist criticized young King Herod for stealing his brother's wife. Therefore both the King and his wife, Herodias, hated and wanted to kill John.

↓ Event 88

R-Rated story:

Young King Herod Antipas (son of Herod the Great) killed John the Baptist

References in the Bible

Matthew 14:11-12

His head was brought in on a dish and given to the girl (Herod Antipas' daughter), who carried it to her mother.

Mark 6:21-29

Luke 9:7-9

More elaborations

Nowadays some churches even have children reenacting this tragic story. What was in the mind of church leaders?

Meanwhile people even criticize some food and travel shows for showing the chef killing live chickens or live seafood.

Event 89
Jesus claims to be the Son of God

References in the Bible

John 5:16-30

Very truly I tell you, the Son can do nothing by himself; he can do only what he sees his father doing, because whatever the Father does the Son also does.

More elaborations

Jesus only said that God was his father. Jesus did not say "I am God". There is a big difference between Father and Son. We all knew that through our own life.

Event 90
Jesus feeds 5,000 with just 5 loaves of bread and 2 fish

References in the Bible

Matthew 14:18-20

They all ate and were satisfied, and the disciples picked up 12 basketfuls of broken pieces that were left over.

Mark 6:35-44

Luke 9:10-17

John 6:1-15

More elaborations

With the homeless issue that we are now facing perhaps ***Jesus the Second*** can help when he comes down to Earth again!

Event 91
Jesus walks on water

References in the Bible
Matthew 14:25
Shortly before dawn Jesus went out to them, walking on the lake.

Mark 6:47-50

John 6:16-21

More elaborations
Poor Peter! He wanted to duplicate Jesus' God-like power but almost drowned for trying. His weakness was the lack of faith.

Event 92

Jesus healed those who touch him

References in the Bible

Matthew 14:36

People brought all who were ill to him and begged him to let those who were ill just touch the edge of his cloak, and all who touched it were healed.

Mark 6:53-56

More elaborations

Jesus was known to have power within him but people with a strong faith could even benefit just by touching Jesus' coat.

Many times Jesus told the people who were healed that their faith actually healed themselves, not by Jesus directly.

↑ Event 93
Jesus tries hard to convince his followers

References in the Bible
John 6:22-59
I am the bread of life. Whoever comes to me will never go hungry, and whoever believes in me will never be thirsty.

Whoever eats this bread will live forever. This bread is my flesh which I will give to the life of the world.

More elaborations
Only John recorded this part of Jesus struggling within himself. How could he convince all followers about him being God's only son?

The concept of "live forever" might not be understood by Jesus' followers. They assumed their existing life would last forever.

Event 94
Many disciples desert Jesus

References in the Bible

John 6:60-71

From this time many of disciples turned back and no longer followed him.

Have I not chosen you, the Twelve? Yet one of you is a devil!

More elaborations

It must have been a sad day for Jesus, seeing his followers leaving him. However knowing one of the Twelve would betray him was a big blow to Jesus' heart.

Event 95
Jesus teaches about inner purity

References in the Bible

Matthew 15:2

Why do your disciples break the tradition of the elders? They don't wash their hands before they eat!

Mark 7:1-5

Luke 11:37-41

More elaborations

Surely Jesus' disciples were wrong by not washing their hands, but Jesus thought their sin was small compared to the Pharisees' sin in neglecting their parents for the sake of serving God (by devoting all money and resources to the temple).

Event 96
Jesus teaches about the words that come out of our mouth

References in the Bible

<u>Matthew 15:18-20</u>

But the things that come out of a person's mouth come from the heart, and these (words) defile them (the speakers).

<u>Mark 7:20-23</u>

More elaborations

Jesus thought a person who spoke bad words were dirtier than his disciples who did not wash their hands before eating.

Event 97

Jesus chases the demon out of a Gentile girl

References in the Bible

Matthew 15:28

Then Jesus said to her, "Woman you have great faith! Your request is granted." And her daughter was healed at that moment.

Mark 7:24-30

The woman was Greek, born in Syrian Phoenicia. She begged Jesus to drive the demon out of her daughter.

More elaborations

Jesus' main mission was to save the Jews. Back in those days the Gentile people were considered as "dogs", not a priority. Still, Jesus helped her because this Canaanite woman had deep faith in Jesus.

Event 98
Jesus heals the masses

References in the Bible

Matthew 15:29-31

The people were amazed when they saw the mute speaking, the crippled made well, the lame walking, and the blind seeing.

Mark 7:31

More elaborations

Actually, even after his death, Jesus continued to heal millions of people especially those with a broken spirit. Lacking clear direction in life and faith in God has brought people down on their knees. Only Jesus can save our broken world.

Event 99
Jesus feeds 4,000 men plus women and children with just 7 loaves of bread and a few fish

References in the Bible

Matthew 15:36

Then he took the seven loaves and the fish, and when he had given thanks, he broke them and gave them to the disciples, and they in turn to the people.

Mark 8:1-10

More elaborations

That was the second time Jesus fed a big crowd with a few loaves of bread and a few fish. Not sure how the fish were prepared or cooked?

Event 100
Jewish leaders ask Jesus to give them a sign

References in the Bible
Matthew 16:1-4
A wicked and adulterous generation looks for a sign, but none will be given it except the sign of Jonah.

Mark 8:13

More elaborations
Jesus himself was the sign but those Pharisees and Sadducees were too blind to see!

Note: The story of Jonah, a man who was in the stomach of a fish for three days, but came out alive (Jesus gave them a hint about his resurrection).

Event 101

Jesus warns his disciple about the wrong teaching of Pharisees and Sadducees, using yeast as a metaphor

References in the Bible

Matthew 16:12

Then they (disciples) understood that he (Jesus) was not telling them to guard against the yeast used in bread but against the teaching of Pharisees and Sadducees.

Mark 8:14   Luke 12:1-12

More elaborations

Like God, his father, Jesus dislikes yeast or refers to it as something bad or impure. However he hates hypocrisy even more. The Pharisees and Sadducees were two political groups ruling the Jews during the times of Jesus. These upper-class leaders benefited from their policies and teachings that made the rest of the population their slaves.

Event 102

Jesus restores sight of a blind man

References in the Bible

Mark 8:22-26

Once more Jesus put his hands on the man's eyes. Then his eyes opened, his sight was restored, and he saw everything clearly.

More elaborations

There were a few incidences when Jesus restored the sight of the blind. We should think beyond the physical blindness and look at our mental blindness as well.

Perhaps we can use Jesus' help to restore our sight, which is often blocked by money, power, or lust.

Event 103

Jesus asks Peter "who do you say I am?"

References in the Bible

Matthew 16:16

Simon Peter answered, "You are the Messiah, the Son of the Living God."

Matthew 16:19

I will give you the keys of the kingdom of heaven; whatever you bind on earth will be bound in heaven, and whatever you loose on earth will be loosed in heaven.

Mark 8:27   Luke 9:18-20

More elaborations

Jesus confirmed he was a Messiah with Peter but told him not to tell anyone else.

Jesus also promised to give Peter the keys to heaven! I guess Jesus forgot that Peter would later deny knowing him, not just once but three times.

↑ Event 104
Jesus predicts his death to his disciples, for the first time (and scolds Peter for talking him out of it)

References in the Bible

Matthew 16:21

Jesus began to explain to his disciples that he must go to Jerusalem and suffer many things before the hands of the elders, the chief priests and the teachers of the law, and that he must be killed and on the third day be raised to life.

Jesus turned and said to Peter, "Get behind me, Satan! You are a stumbling block to me; you do not have in mind the concerns of God, but merely human concerns."

Mark 8:31   Luke 9:21-27

More elaborations

Come to think of it: Jesus was not killed by drunk drivers, by gangsters, by gun owners, or by war. Jesus was killed by the Religious Leaders!

Don't be an extremist or fanatic for any religion! I would rather be friends with an atheist than an extreme God-loving fanatic.

Poor Peter, first Jesus promised him the keys to Heaven then called him Satan right after!

Event 105
Jesus is transfigured on the mountain

References in the Bible

Matthew 17:2-8

There he (Jesus) was transfigured before them. His face shone like the sun, and his clothes became as white as light. Just then tree appeared before them (Peter, John and James) Moses and Elijah, talking with Jesus.

Mark 9:2

Luke 9:28

More elaborations

How did Peter recognize Moses and Elijah who also appeared with Jesus? Were there photos of them posted somewhere?

Event 106

Jesus knows John the Baptist is Elijah (a prophet that God had sent down in the past)

References in the Bible

<u>Matthew 17:12</u>

But I tell you, Elijah has already come, and they did not recognize him, but have done to him everything the wished (harming ways).

More elaborations

John the Baptist, also known as Elijah failed to save the Jews. Not sure why Jesus thought he could do better?

In a way, the fact that Elijah died and then came back as John the Baptist is the proof that Jesus believed in reincarnation.

Event 107
Jesus heals a demon-possessed boy

References in the Bible

Matthew 17:18

Jesus rebuked the demon and it came out of the boy, and he was healed at that moment.

Mark 9:17-29

This kind (driving out demon) can come out by prayer.

Luke 9:37-41

I begged your disciples to drive it out but they could not.

"You unbelieving and perverse generation", Jesus replied, "how long shall I stay with you and put up with you? Bring your son here."

More elaborations

Jesus was not happy with his disciples for failing to heal the boy themselves.

No surprise to me! These disciples actually did not want to learn much from Jesus. They hopped on the bandwagon with their only hope in gaining power through the Ministry of Jesus, like a position in the government.

Event 108
Jesus predicts his death for the second time

References in the Bible
Matthew 17:22-23
They will kill him (me/Jesus), and on the third day he will be raised to life.

Mark 9:30

Luke 9:44

More elaborations
Jesus' disciples only heard clearly the first part that Jesus would be killed. They either missed the second part completely or had no idea about the resurrection.

If I was Jesus' adviser I would have asked Jesus not to reveal too much about his imminent death. The followers hated to hear that their leader would be prosecuted and killed very soon.

↔ Event 109

Jesus solves the argument among the disciples, who is the best?

References in the Bible

Matthew 18:2

He called the little child to him and placed the child among them. And he said: "Truly I tell you, unless you change and become like little children, you will never enter the kingdom of heaven."

Mark 9:33-37

Luke 9:46

Jesus, knowing their thoughts, took a little child and made him stand beside him.

More elaborations

Another inconsistent detail of where the child was placed. Matthew mentioned "placed the child among them" while Luke said "make him (the child) stand beside him (Jesus)".

This argument between the disciples also showed that none of them was any good. Only Jesus with a big and good heart could forgive the disciples but most of us would not accept their childish mentality and selfishness. What a shame!

Event 110

Jesus is OK with someone using his name to drive out demons (John, his disciple, does not like it)

References in the Bible

Mark 9:38

Do not stop him, Jesus said. For no one who does a miracle in my name can in the next moment say anything bad about me.

Luke 9:49-50

More elaborations

Very good logic! If someone does good things and gives us the credit then we should embrace that generous gesture. John the disciple was perhaps jealous since he could not do the same.

Event 111
Jesus expects full commitment from his disciples

References in the Bible
Luke 14:25-33
Suppose one of you wants to build a tower. Won't you first sit down and estimate the cost to see if you have enough money to complete it?"

More elaborations
You have to carry the cross for Jesus until the end. As it turned out, none of the disciples did!

Like the disciples of Jesus, most of us don't always have a full commitment when we start a new project or chase after a dream.

↑ Event 112
Jesus warns against temptation

References in the Bible
Matthew 18:7-9
If your hand or your foot causes you to stumble, cut it off and throw it away. It is better for you to enter life maimed or crippled than to have two hands or two feet and be thrown into eternal fire.

Mark 9:42-49

More elaborations
Next to **Event 39** or **Lesson 4** about serving God and Money, this teaching from Jesus is as important. We should avoid the temptation at all cost. Also, we must not be the ones who tempt others, especially children into doing the sinful acts. Both are bad to the eyes of Jesus.

We spend all our life trying to obtain or accumulate tangibles that we believe will make our life more complete. With that mentality we easily get trapped or fall into the temptation.

Before we can enter the Kingdom of God or just a stage of happiness, we must learn to get rid of the tangibles that have been harming us.

↑ Event 113

Jesus tells us to respect and treat children kindly

References in the Bible

Matthew 18:10

See that you do not despise one of these little ones. For I tell you that their angels in heaven always see the face of my Father in heaven.

More elaborations

As adults we too have angels guarding us but the angles of children are God's buddies. They have higher authority!

Please do not mistake Jesus' word of "despite" with teach or guide. Many times we have seen young children running wild and screaming out loud during the Sunday services in the church. We wish either their parents or someone from the church would control the bad behavior of those children.

Event 114

Jesus teaches how to correct your loved ones

References in the Bible

Matthew 18:15

If your brother or sister sins, go and point out their fault, just between the two of you. If they listen to you, you have won them over.

More elaborations

Go easy first, then hard later if the sinner keeps ignoring our help. This lesson applies to strangers as well. However, when facing with the confrontation we tend to do the opposite of what Jesus teaches us. We quickly turn away from the issue in hatred or resentment. Very few of us would try our best to help the offenders or to rebuild the relationship.

Event 115
Jesus tells Peter how to forgive his loved ones for sinning against him

References in the Bible

Matthew 18:21

Then Peter came to Jesus and asked. "Lord, how many times should I forgive my brother or sister who sins against me? Up to seven times?"

Luke 17:3-4

Even if they sin against you seven times in a day and seven times to come back to you saying "I repent", you must forgive them.

More elaborations

This part of Jesus' teaching is the concept of "paying forward". The one who received the favor (being forgiven in this story) should do the same for others.

Also, very often we could not return the favor to the people who helped us in the past. The best way to give back is to copy their kindness by doing favors to others later in life.

↑ Event 116
Jesus tells the story of a Good Samaritan

References in the Bible
Luke 10:25-37
A man was going down from Jerusalem to Jericho, when he was attacked by robbers. They stripped him of his clothes, beat him and went away, leaving him half-dead.

More elaborations
Only Luke had this good moral story. People nowadays hate to be involved in a bad situation where their own wellbeing or reputation may be harmed. The word "Samaritan" has become the synonym of kind people, well deserved!

What is the point being made here? Jesus used the Parable of the Good Samaritan as example of humanity at its best. If a Samaritan could rise above the bigotry and prejudices for centuries by showing mercy and compassion for the injured Jew, after the Jew's own countrymen passed him by, then why couldn't we do the same? Is our human value lower than the Samaritans'?

Event 117

Jesus visits Martha and Mary (*the same Mary who later pours expensive perfume on Jesus' feet)*

References in the Bible

Luke 10:38-42

Lord, don't you care if my sister (Mary) has left me to do the work by myself? Tell her to help me!

More elaborations

Only Luke had this guest-hosting story. Two sisters, two skills, and two personalities! Mary was better at hosting so being with Jesus was the right place for her. Poor Martha! She was a good cook and a good organizer so she was stuck in the kitchen!

↑ Event 118

Jesus teaches his disciples how to pray, for the second time

References in the Bible

Luke 11:1-13

Father, hallowed be your name, your kingdom come. Give us each day our daily bread. Forgive our sins, for we also forgive everyone who sins against us. And lead us not into temptation.

More elaborations

Only Luke had this teaching, a good way to pray. This is known as The Lord's Prayer and its wording is varied by different Christian denominations.

Why do we need to pray? Remember that there is *no free lunch.* You want something then prepare to give back something. God is always generous to us but don't take the love of our Lord for granted.

We all have heard the expression *"there are no atheists in foxholes".* When exposed to the extreme danger many people reflect on the spiritual or supernatural dimension of existence.

"*We also forgive everyone who sins against us*" is the highlight of this prayer. Forgiveness is our gift for God.

Event 119

Jesus criticizes the religious leaders

References in the Bible

Luke 11:42-54

And you experts in the law, woe to you, because you load people down with burdens they can hardly carry, and you yourself will not lift one finger to help them.

More elaborations

Criticizing someone directly especially in front of others is not a good way to correct the offenders. No wonder Jesus had so many enemies in the temples and synagogues!

In any society religious and political leaders are almost untouchable. Anyone who dared to expose the corruptions mostly ended up dead, by crucifying, assassinating, or poisoning.

Event 120

Jesus' own brothers ridicule him

References in the Bible

John 7:4-5

"No one who wants to become a public figure acts in secret. Since you are doing these things, show yourself to the world." For even his own brothers did not believe in him.

More elaborations

John (the writer/Jesus' disciple) continued to show the lack of belief in Jesus, even from his own brothers. They only began to believe Jesus after the resurrection. Later in life some of them even became leaders in the church.

Event 121
Jesus comes (secretly) and teaches at the temple

References in the Bible

John 7:10-31

At that point some of the people of Jerusalem began to ask, "Isn't it the man they tried to kill? Here he is, speaking publicly, and they are not saying a word to him."

More elaborations

Jesus could only convince some, not all people of Jerusalem, especially the religious leaders. They did not believe Jesus was the son of God.

Event 122

Religious leaders try to arrest Jesus

References in the Bible

John 7:32-52

Nicodemus, who had gone to Jesus earlier and who was one of their own number (religious leaders/Pharisees), asked, "Does our law condemn a man without hearing him to find out what he has been doing?"

More elaborations

Jesus used God as a backup for his teachings and actions, but that approach did not work well with the Pharisees or religious leaders. They could not see beyond the flesh and blood of Jesus himself.

Nicodemus was a good man. He was a religious leader himself but realized how valuable Jesus' teachings were to him and others. He tried his best to protect Jesus from other fanatic religious leaders or the Pharisees.

↑ Event 123
Jesus forgives an adulterous woman

References in the Bible

John 8:1-11

Let anyone of you who is without sin be the first to throw a stone at her.

More elaborations

Only John had this good story about a sinful woman who was about to be stoned. I first heard about this "stoning" story through a college roommate. It gave me a very good impression of Jesus. I started liking him since that time.

Event 124
Jesus continues to fight religious leaders in Jerusalem

References in the Bible

John 8:12

I am the light of the world. Whoever follows me will never walk in darkness, but will have the light of life.

John 8:13-59

Then you will know the truth, and the truth will set you free.

More elaborations

We all knew Jesus had lost this fight against the religious leaders. To lose a fight and his life but to gain billions of followers after his death was a grand victory for Jesus.

We should learn not to jump to conclusions. Time will tell who actually wins or loses!

I have heard people using the phrase "***The truth will set you free***" but I did not realize that phrase came from Jesus. How great!

↕ Event 125

Jesus teaches about marriage and divorce (for the second time)

References in the Bible

Matthew 19:3-12

Some Pharisees came to Jesus and tested him. They asked, "Is it lawful for a man to divorce his wife for any and every reason?"

Mark 10:1-12

Moses permitted a man to write a certificate of divorce and send her away.

More elaborations

Living an unmarried life was acceptable to Jesus. However, Jesus did not approve of divorce, not agreeing with Moses!

Event 126

Jesus warns about the division on Earth

References in the Bible

Luke 12:49-53

From now on there will be five in one family divided against each other, three against two and two against three.

More elaborations

At the moment (the year 2020), our world looks exactly like what had happened back in Jesus' days. Not only are family members divided against each other but the split even goes up to the government level. States disagree with other states and at the same time political parties attack each other. Furthermore, one country is trying to destroy the other.

The same division is still on Earth even after 2,000 years, and perhaps will be the same for 10,000 more years.

Event 127

Jesus warns about the conflict among us

References in the Bible

Luke 12:57-59

Why don't you judge for yourself what is right?

More elaborations

Jesus wanted us to resolve conflicts first among ourselves before dragging each other to court.

Have you ever watched the American TV show Judge Judy? It was so sad to see a daughter suing her mother for a small piece of furniture.

Event 128
Jesus wants the people to repent

References in the Bible
Luke 13:1-5
Do you think that these Galileans were worse sinners than all the other Galileans because they suffered this way? I tell you, no! But unless you repent, you too will all perish.

More elaborations
The Romans killed many Galilean workers since Pilate thought they rebelled against him and his Roman government.

These workers were actually helping the Romans to build the aqueduct. Jesus did not condemn anyone, but warned us that we would have the same fate if we did not repent.

Event 129

Jesus healed a crippled woman on the Sabbath

References in the Bible

Luke 13:10-17

Then he put his hands on her, and immediately she straightened up and praised God.

There are six days for work. So come and be healed on those days, not on the Sabbath (statement from Synagogue).

More elaborations

Jesus again involved in another conflict with the religious leaders for working on the Sabbath!

You can understand why. The religious leaders have been busy collecting gifts and wine on "those six days". They need to have a free day to enjoy their collections!

Event 130
Jesus talks about the Kingdom of God, for the first time

References in the Bible

Luke 13:18-21

It is like a mustard seed, which a man took and planted in his garden. It grew and became a tree and the birds perched on its branches.

More elaborations

His followers, especially the 12 disciples were expecting a big palace on earth with a huge government which they could be a part of.

Event 131
Jesus heals a man with swollen limbs on the Sabbath

References in the Bible

Luke 14:1-6

If you have a child or an ox that falls into a well on Sabbath day, will you not immediately pull it out?

More elaborations

The extremists were everywhere, especially in the temples. They faulted Jesus for "working" on the Sabbath. Until the late 1990s, most businesses in Australia were not allowed to open on Sunday.

↑ Event 132

Jesus teaches about seeking honors

References in the Bible

Luke 14:7-14

For those who exalt themselves will be humbled, and those who humbled themselves will be exalted.

When you give a luncheon or dinner, do not invite your friends, your brothers or sisters, your relatives, or your rich neighbors; if you do, they may invite you back and so you will be repaid.

More elaborations

You should try to read all verses of this subject. Jesus taught us to be humble because under God's view we would be honored. The opposite is also true.

This teaching does not go well with the super-rich people who have big banquets every weekend so that they can show off their wealth to others. Also, through these lavish parties the rich folks hope to gain more opportunities to make themselves even richer.

Although I think God would have approved of them if they had invited the homeless and the poor as their guests.

↑ Event 133
Jesus tells the parable of the lost sheep and the lost silver coin

References in the Bible

Luke 15:1-10

I tell you that in the same way there will be more rejoicing in heaven over one sinner who repents than over ninety-nine righteous people who do not need repent.

More elaborations

How ironic! Have you heard the phrase "*the squeaky wheel gets the grease*"? We don't pay much attention to those good wheels. Through this we can see that Jesus is also human!

Event 134

Jesus tells the parable about the lost son

References in the Bible

<u>Luke 15:11-32</u>

But we had to celebrate and be glad, because this brother of yours was dead and is alive again; he was lost and is found.

More elaborations

Not a fair treatment to the good son! Again, the squeaky wheel gets the grease! Actually, this is about the recruiting process. We only need to spend money to court the “non-believer”. There is no need to spend the money on the ones who already believed. Ouch!

Event 135

Jesus tells the parable of the shrewd manager

References in the Bible

Luke 16:1-12

Whoever can be trusted with very little can also be trusted with much, and whoever is dishonest with very little will also be dishonest with much.

More elaborations

Business deals seldom bring good friendships. The shrewd manager made deals to gain favors from his customers at the expense of his boss.

Event 136

Jesus tells the story of a rich man and the beggar

References in the Bible

Luke 16:19-31

Son (the rich man), remember that in your lifetime you received your good things, while Lazarus (the beggar) received bad things, but now he is comforted here and you are in agony.

More elaborations

Have you seen the movie titled "Trading Places" with Dan Aykroyd and Eddie Murphy?

Will I turn into a noble man when I become rich? Or will I turn into a thief when I am poor?

↑ Event 137
Jesus warns the predators who may hurt children

References in the Bible

Luke 17:1-3

It would be better for them to be thrown into the sea with a millstone tied around their neck than to cause one of those little ones to stumble.

More elaborations

The predators are everywhere. They could be in school, church, or next door. They could even hurt the children from another country via the Internet!

↑ Event 138
Jesus healed ten men with leprosy, but only one thanked him

References in the Bible
Luke 17:11-19
Has no one returned to give praise to God except this foreigner?

More elaborations
Back in Jesus' times, the Samaritans appeared to be more decent than the Jews. Perhaps they lived in a more peaceful time when things were easy to get.

We are busy people, especially the 21st century human race. Most of us use shortcuts trying to be in front of others even just for a second. No one has time to turn around and give thanks to people who have helped us.

↑ Event 139

Jesus talks about the Kingdom of God, the second time

References in the Bible

<u>Luke 17:20-37</u>

The coming of the kingdom of God is not something that can be observed, nor will people say, "Here it is", or "There it is", because the kingdom of God is in your midst.

I tell you, on that night two people will be on one bed; one will be taken and the other left.

More elaborations

At the time of this writing, the Covid-19 or Coronavirus is hitting the world. Some people have begun to talk about the Second Coming of Jesus. If not the real coming then I think this pandemic is a solid warning from God to humanity. Many powerful countries with nuclear weapons were brought to their knees.

"Kingdom of God is in your midst"? Jesus wanted us to search for it within ourselves. Very deep teaching!

Event 140

Jesus tells the story of a persistent widow

References in the Bible

Luke 18:1-8

Even though I don't fear God or care what people think, yet because this widow keeps bothering me, I will see that she gets justice, so that she won't eventually come and attack me.

More elaborations

Being persistent pays off sometimes. Well, you can try to nag God for something that you want!

As for the judge, he was very smart for not trying to upset this desperate widow further.

↑ Event 141
Jesus blessed the children, again

References in the Bible

Matthew 19:14

Let the little children come to me, and do not hinder them, for the kingdom of heaven belongs to such as these.

Mark 10:13-16

Luke 18:15-17

More elaborations

Jesus again lectured to his disciples about the importance of being children. Our politicians have learned this lesson well from Jesus. While campaigning, they always hold or hug a few cute babies for photo opportunities.

↑ Event 142

Jesus again teaches about being rich and being accepted in the Kingdom of God

References in the Bible

Matthew 19:24

Again I tell you, it is easier for a camel to go through the eye of the needle than for someone who is rich to enter the kingdom of God.

Mark 10:17

Luke 18:18

More elaborations

Bill Gates and Jeff Bezos, are you reading this? Although Bill and Jeff already entered their own kingdom of US Dollars so perhaps they don't care much about the Kingdom of God.

To their credit, both have donated billions to worthy causes. Still, year after year we continue to see their names listed as the richest people on Earth. Let's hope that in their wills they already have pledged to give all away to the poor!

Event 143

Jesus reassures Peter for giving up everything to follow Jesus

References in the Bible

Matthew 19:27

We have left everything to follow you! What then will be there for us?

Mark 10:28

More elaborations

Peter cared only for himself. No wonder he denied Jesus three times when Jesus got into trouble.

After spending two years to follow Jesus, Peter began to lose patience. The Kingdom was still not seen nor was his reward. Peter perhaps was a good fisherman but he for sure did not have the virtues of a fruit-tree farmer. After the seeds were planted, it would take years before the farmer could harvest any fruit.

Event 144

Jesus teaches about "capitalism", from the vineyard owner's point-of-view

References in the Bible

Matthew 20:13-15

Didn't you agree to work for a denarius? Take your pay and go. I want to give the one who was hired last the same as I gave you.

More elaborations

There is no fairness in life, neither then nor now. The boss always has the right to treat employees differently, in any business!

Having the products ready by day's end is important to the boss. He or she may have to bring in temps or pay overtime to workers so that the products would be delivered on time. Profit is the top priority for the boss, not the fairness for his or her employees.

Event 145

Jesus predicts his death the third time

References in the Bible

Matthew 20:18-20

We are going up to Jerusalem, and the Son of Man will be delivered over to the chief priests and the teacher of the law.

Mark 10:32

Luke 18:31

More elaborations

Was there an alternative course of life for Jesus? Perhaps there was, but no one dared or cared enough to suggest it to Jesus.

Event 146

Jesus teaches about the importance of serving others, not to be served

References in the Bible

Matthew 20:21

Grant that one of these two sons of mine (James and John are Jesus' cousins) may sit at your right and the other at your left.

Mark 10:35

More elaborations

Mom always wants the best for her sons, especially since they are not only disciples, but also cousins of Jesus.

Mark wrote that James and John, not their mother, asked Jesus for the seats at his left and right.

Event 147
Rift among the disciples

References in the Bible
<u>Mark 10:41</u>
When the ten (disciples) heard about this (the request of sitting next to Jesus in heaven), they became indignant with James and John.

More elaborations
Can't blame the "ten" for being upset by the greedy brothers, James and John! Although most of these disciples thought Jesus would have an earthly kingdom.

↕ Event 148

Jesus heals the man who was born blind

References in the Bible

John 9:1-34

His disciples asked him (Jesus), "Rabbi, who sinned, this man or his parents, that he was born blind?"

"Neither this man nor his parents sinned", said Jesus.

More elaborations

If you have read **Event 61,** about a paralyzed man who was healed by Jesus then you would remember the first thing Jesus did was to forgive the man' sin. This time Jesus said that there was no sin committed by either the blind man or by his parents. Is there a conflict in Jesus teachings here?

Perhaps Jesus was looking at the big picture by telling his disciples that the blindness was not the result of the sin (karma) the man or his parents committed. In Jesus' point of view, it was merely an opportunity for him to do God's work.

Event 149
Religious leaders question the blind man who was healed by Jesus

References in the Bible

John 9:13-41

"We know he is our son." The parents answered, "and we knew he was born blind. But how he can see now, or who opened his eyes, we don't know."

More elaborations

The Pharisees had trouble believing that Jesus had healed the man who was born blind. They wanted to find out if the man was actually born blind by pressing his parents for the truth.

Event 150
Jesus heals two blind beggars

References in the Bible
Matthew 20:34
Jesus had compassion on them and touched their eyes. Immediately they received their sight and followed him.

Mark 10:46

Luke 18:35

More elaborations
These two blind men heard Jesus and his entourage going by so they asked Jesus to cure their blindness. Instead of brushing them aside like his disciples had done to the blind men, Jesus decided to stop and heal them. Caring for others perhaps was Jesus' strongest character or trait

↑ Event 151
Jesus brings salvation to Zacchaeus

References in the Bible

Luke 19:1-10

Look, Lord! Here and now I give half of my possessions to the poor, and if I have cheated anybody out of anything, I will pay back four times the amount.

More elaborations

It is never too late to do the right thing! Thanks to Jesus, this man, who certainly had not lived a sin-free life, decided to give away his wealth to the poor.

He had been feeling free of guilt until Jesus came along. Nothing he could hide from Jesus, especially his wealth and sins!

↕ Event 152

Jesus tells the parable of a King and his servants

References in the Bible

Luke 19:11-26

So he called ten of his servants and gave them ten minas (each). "Put this money to work," he said, "until I come back."

Luke 19: 27

But those enemies of mine who did not want me to be king over them – bring them here and kill them in front of me.

More elaborations

Jesus brought up a good example of doing extra in life especially in the current highly competitive world. Just keeping the 10 minas as told by the King was not good enough.

"Ân Dền Oán Trả", a Vietnamese proverb means "returning favors to the ones who helped us but punishing the ones who hurt us."

What happened to Jesus' teaching about anger and forgiveness? Very sure the King in this story has never heard of the man named Jesus!

↔ Event 153
Jesus rides a donkey to Jerusalem

References in the Bible

Matthew 21: 1-11

The disciples went and did as Jesus had instructed them. They brought the donkey and the colt and placed their cloaks on them for Jesus to sit on.

Mark 11:1-11

Luke 19:28-44

John 12:12-19

More elaborations

Just a donkey or a donkey and her colt? Two different details were recorded by two authors. Mark' story makes more sense since Jesus can only ride on one.

↑ Event 154

Jesus clears the temple, again

References in the Bible

Matthew 21:12

Jesus entered the temple court and drove out all who were buying and selling there.

Mark 11:15

Luke 19:45-46

My house will be a house of prayer. But you have made it into a den of robbers.

More elaborations

No religious commercial? Selling doves is not as bad as selling drug or sex!

Jesus himself did not even have a fixed or permanent shelter where he could call home or church. But if we look around we may notice some huge churches or temples that are worth millions of dollars. Well, Jesus did not like marketing because he only served God!

Event 155

Jesus teaches about the power of prayer (the poor fig tree!)

References in the Bible

Matthew 21:18

May you never bear fruit again! Immediately the tree withered.

Matthew 21:22

If you believe, you will receive whatever you ask for in prayer.

Mark 11:12 & 11:20

More elaborations

Jesus killed the innocent fig tree. How impatient Jesus was! No one should expect the tree would always bear fruits.

The same impatient Jesus who once praised Peter and promised to give him the keys to Heaven but then right after that scolded Peter and called him "Satan". See **Events 103** and **104**.

Event 156

Religious leaders challenge Jesus' authority

References in the Bible

Matthew 21:23-37

By what authority are you doing these things?

Mark 12:27-33

Luke 20:1-8

More elaborations

The old establishment did not like the new guy named Jesus!

We could understand why since Jesus' teaching did not make the temples or synagogues any richer. He also spent no effort to make those religious leaders more powerful.

↑ Event 157

Jesus warns the non-believers

References in the Bible

Matthew 21:31-32

Truly I tell you, the tax collectors and the prostitutes are entering the kingdom of God ahead of you (the non-believers).

More elaborations

Poor IRS (USA) and ATO (Australia) personnel! They were grouped with the prostitutes as sinners. Just wonder where Jesus would group our politicians?

↓ Event 158

Jesus uses the metaphor of God being the Landowner and humans as the tenants

References in the Bible

Matthew 21:43

Therefore I tell you that the kingdom of God will be taken away from you and given to a people who will produce its fruits.

Mark 12:1-12

Luke 20:9-19

He will come and kill the tenants and give the vineyard to others.

More elaborations

We are not doing a good job in taking care of our planet at the moment. It is easy to move on to the next place and forget the current one.

Over the course of our lifetime we each have had at least a dozen places called home, either rental or our own. For some of us, those places even spread out to many continents. Still, we are on the same planet, the only one.

Always be a good caretaker of your place, regardless of the ownership and regardless of the stay duration.

Event 159
Jesus teaches about being considered (as wedding guests)

References in the Bible
Matthew 22:11-14
For many are invited, but few are chosen.

Luke 14:16-24
I tell you, not one of those who were invited will get a taste of my banquet.

More elaborations
Don't take anything for granted! Once you have accepted the invitation, you had to make yourself presentable.

↑ Event 160

Jesus was asked about paying taxes

References in the Bible

Matthew 22:17

Tell us then, what is your opinion? Is it right to pay the imperial (poll) tax to Caesar or not?

Mark 12:13-17

Luke 20:20-25

Then give back to Caesar what is Caesar's, and to God what is God's.

More elaborations

According to Luke, Jesus told us that we should pay tax to the government but don't forget to give the money to the church also!

Life is all about double duties. To be successful you must master your juggling skills, to handle more than one thing at once. Being a good father or mother to your children is not enough. You must be a good son or daughter to your parents also. That's a double duty!

Event 161

Jesus answers about resurrection or afterlife

References in the Bible

Matthew 22:23-32

At the resurrection people will neither marry nor be given in marriage; they will be like angels in heaven.

Mark 12:18-27

At the resurrection whose wife will she be, since seven were married to her?

Luke 20:27-38

More elaborations

Interesting woman with seven husbands who all were brothers! She was the first black widow.

Not sure how true this story is. I can't imagine there is a family with seven brothers who all died and left this poor woman alone.

Poor Jesus too! He had to answer a very tough question. Soon, we all will know how true his answer is (seeing Jesus after our own death).

Event 162

Jesus teaches about the greatest Commandment

References in the Bible

Matthew 22:37

Love the Lord your God with all your heart and with all your soul and with all your mind.

Mark 12:28

More elaborations

We only love God with all our heart during the hard times, when things are going wrong or when we are in trouble. Otherwise, God is just a convenient name that we mention now and then. Like an insurance policy that we need to hold on to for the protection but have no need to read every single line.

↑ Event 163
Jesus warns against religious leaders

References in the Bible

Matthew 23:2-3

So you must be careful to do everything they tell you. But do not do what they do, for they do not practice what they preach.

Mark 12:38

Luke 20:45-47

They (religious leaders) devour widows' houses and for a show make lengthy prayers. These men will be punished most severely.

More elaborations

It was true 2,000 years ago and it is still true now. Religious leaders don't do windows! All hard work is done by devoted nuns and followers.

Having a priest sitting at the VIP table in our living room during a party is a big honor. We were trained to look at priests and monks as God, without checking their references. Meanwhile, we do a thorough check of our potential gardener!

↑ Event 164
A poor widow gives all she has

References in the Bible

Mark 12:43

Truly I tell you, this poor widow has put more into the treasury than all the others. They all gave out of their wealth; but she, out of her poverty, put in everything – all she has to live on.

Luke 21:1-4

More elaborations

Relatively speaking of course! A million dollars is like a treasure for most of us but that amount is only valued as pennies to the billionaires.

↑ Event 165
Jesus tells us not calling anyone on earth "Father"

References in the Bible

Matthew 23:9

And do not call anyone on earth "father", for you have one Father, and he is in heaven.

More elaborations

Ever wonder why the Catholic folks do not follow Jesus' teaching about using the "Father" term. It is weird to hear an older man or woman calling a much younger priest "Father". Minister is a respectable term.

Mayor is an honorable term for the head of a city. However several English-speaking countries even add the term "Lord" to the title Mayor as "Lord Mayor". I think Lord should be used for God only.

Event 166

Jesus condemns the religious leaders

References in the Bible

Matthew 23:13-36

You (religious leaders) say, "if anyone who swears by the temple, it means nothing, but if anyone who swears by the gold of the temple is bound by that oath."

More elaborations

Over time, even with good intentions at the beginning, most churches would turn out to be more like a corporate or business center. Over 500 years ago a German Christian named Martin Luther did point out the troubles with the churches and church leaders. Wealth does not buy us a seat or "sky-box" in heaven.

Event 167

Jesus grieves over Jerusalem

References in the Bible

Matthew 23:37

Jerusalem, you who kill the prophets and stone those sent to you, how often I have longed to gather your children together, as a hen gathers her chicks under her wings, and you are not willing.

Luke 13:31-35

More elaborations

Jesus loved the capital of God's chosen people but sadly the people of Jerusalem did not care for him or his teaching. The rest of the world believed and repented to Jesus but after 2,000 years most people of Jerusalem still have not gotten the message.

Event 168

Jesus predicts the future of earthlings

References in the Bible

Matthew 24:3-7

Nation will rise against nation, and kingdom against kingdom. There will be famines and earthquakes in various places.

Mark 13:1-23

Luke 21:5-24

More elaborations

Jesus promised to come back, but warned of the phonies who claimed themselves to be Jesus or The Messiah. How will we see the difference? Surely Jesus will not appear in Israel again as the last time he was there things did not turn out well for him.

Event 169
Jesus talks about his glorious return

References in the Bible

Matthew 24:31

And he will send his angels with a loud trumpet call, and they will gather his elect from the four winds, from one end of the heavens to the other.

Mark 13:24

Luke 21:25

More elaborations

This message from Jesus seems to be either too advanced or out of place. Jesus was still alive and preaching. Why would he talk about his return?

Of course he already told his disciples about his coming death, but that event still had not happened. Therefore, none of his disciples had any idea about this promise from Jesus. He had not left at that time so the discussion about his return did not make any sense to the disciples.

Event 170

Jesus tells us to be vigilant since his return will be a very quick appearance

References in the Bible

Matthew 24:42

Therefore keep watching, because you do not know on what day your Lord will come.

Mark 13:35   Luke 12:35-40

It would be good for those servants whose master finds them watching when he comes.

Luke 21:34-36

When these things begin to take place, stand up and lift up your heads, because your redemption is drawing near.

More elaborations

Jesus continued to talk about his return and especially warned about the suddenness of his re-appearance. If you blink, you will miss Jesus' return!

At the time of this writing, the Covid-19 pandemic is doing a good job of readjusting the mentality of mankind, one country at a time. Perhaps this is a preview for Jesus' return. The lockdown and quarantine changed my mind about priorities in life. Tiger Woods is no longer a big deal to me. Instead, the delivery guy from the local supermarket is now my new hero!

Event 171
Jesus tells the parable of ten virgins (bridesmaids)

References in the Bible

Matthew 25:1-13

But while they (the 5 "fool" virgins) were on their way to buy the oil, the groom arrived. The virgins who were ready went in with him to the wedding banquet. And the door was shut.

More elaborations

It was the original reality show of the Bachelor!

Bravo to Jesus for not mentioning the hair color of the dumb virgins. Anyway, having the lamps without oil was a result of bad planning.

↕ Event 172

Jesus tells the parable of the gold keepers

References in the Bible

<u>Matthew 25:15</u>

To one he gave 5 bags of gold, to another 2 bags, and to another 1 bag, each according to his ability (to keep).

<u>Luke 19:11-26</u>

[Similar story was recorded by Luke here, except Luke mentioned money "minas" instead].

More elaborations

Not a nice story about the poor servant who did what he was told!

The point Jesus tried to make was about our competitive world. Doing your job alone is not good enough. You have to understand the unspoken words of what your boss really wanted you to do, beyond the job description.

Event 173

Jesus tells about the final judgement

References in the Bible

Matthew 25:32-46

All the nations will be gathered before him (Jesus), and he will separate one from another as a shepherd separates sheep from the goats. He will put the sheep on his right and the goats on his left.

More elaborations

The Democrats in America should be worried. They are sitting on the left!

Event 174

Jesus raises Lazarus from the dead (Lazarus is brother of Mary and Martha)

References in the Bible

John 11:38-44

Jesus called in a loud voice, "Lazarus, come out!" The dead man came out, his hands and feet wrapped with strips of linen, and a cloth around his face.

More elaborations

Knowing the public was waiting for Jesus to perform a miracle (bringing Lazarus back to life) he had no choice but to ask his father, God, to help him.

↓ Event 175
Religious leaders plan to kill Jesus

References in the Bible

Matthew 26:3

Then the chief priests and the elders of the people assembled in the palace of the high priest, whose name was Caiaphas, and they schemed to arrest Jesus secretly and kill him.

Mark 14:1-2

Luke 22:1-2

John 11:45-57

More elaborations

Just wonder who knew about their plan of killing Jesus? Their violent state of mind is incredible by our 21st century standards. Jesus had not done anything bad against the Jews and non-Jews. He did not even try to overthrow the Roman conqueror. Why kill him?

↑ Event 176

A woman (Mary, Lazarus' sister) pours very expensive perfume on Jesus

References in the Bible

Matthew 26:10-11

The poor you will always have with you, but you will not always have me.

Mark 14:3-9

John 12:1-11

More elaborations

A few disciples objected to this lavish gesture saying that perfume could be sold and the money to be used for the poor. The one who objected the most was Judas Iscariot. He managed the money for Jesus' ministry and he was also known for skimming money for himself.

Event 177
Jesus explains why he must die

References in the Bible

John 12:20-26

Very truly I tell you, unless a grain of wheat falls to the ground and dies, it remains only a single seed.

John 27-29

Then the voice came from heaven, "I have glorified it, and will glorify it again". The crowd that was there and heard it said it had thundered; others said an angel had spoken to him.

More elaborations

The banana plant is a good example of this meaningful transformation. The plant dies when its fruit ripens.

To point out how cruel mankind had become Jesus used his death as proof. Our world has turned out to be a self-serving society.

↑ Event 178
Most people still do not believe in Jesus

References in the Bible

John 12:37

Even after Jesus had performed many signs in their presence, they still would not believe in him.

John 12:42

Yet at the same time many even among the leaders believed in him. But because of the Pharisees they would not openly acknowledge the faith for the fear they would be put out of the synagogue; for they love human praise more than praise from God.

More elaborations

John was the only one who put down this sad fact about faith in Jesus and his teachings. Furthermore, those who believed in Jesus were afraid to acknowledge him due to the fear of losing their important positions.

John also wrote about the praise from humans versus praise from God. Praise from humans means getting attention and rewards for the existing life. Praise from God is something that many people prefer to put aside until they are closer to their final days on Earth.

Event 179

Judas Iscariot agrees to betray Jesus

References in the Bible

Matthew 26:14-16

And asked, "What are you willing to give me if I deliver him (Jesus) to you?" So they counted out for him 30 pieces of silver.

Mark 14:10-11

Luke 22:3-6

More elaborations

Poor Jesus, again! His life and the future of mankind were worth only 30 pieces of silver, or about three thousand US dollars at this current time.

Event 180

Jesus picks the host for his Passover dinner

References in the Bible

Matthew 26:18

He replied, "Go into the city to a certain man and tell him, the Teacher says: my appointed time is near. I am going to celebrate the Passover with my disciples at your house."

Mark 14:10-11

Luke 22:3-6

More elaborations

Just wonder whose house was chosen? The owner must be rich since his second floor has a dining room that is big enough to hold 13 people.

↑ Event 181
Jesus washes the disciples' feet

References in the Bible

John 13:1-20

After that, he poured water into a basin and began to wash his disciples' feet, drying them with the towel that was wrapped around him.

More elaborations

John did not mention the name of the first disciple who had his feet washed by Jesus. Perhaps that was John himself, "the one Jesus loved?"

Washing the feet of guests was the old tradition followed by house owners and hosts. It would be a job for the servant. Jesus wanted to treat his disciples as honorable guests. Washing their feet would leave a good impression that during his life on Earth he cared for his disciples. Jesus also taught them to be humble.

Not sure how Judas Iscariot felt at that moment. He had already taken the money for betraying Jesus!

Event 182

Jesus' last supper with disciples

References in the Bible

Matthew 26:20-28

And while they were eating, he said, "Truly I tell you, one of you will betray me."

Jesus took bread, and when he had given thanks, he broke it and gave it to his disciples, saying, "Take and eat; this is my body."

Mark 14:17-25 Luke 22:14-30 John 13:21-30

More elaborations

Jesus told his disciples that he already knew about Judas' betrayal.

Using bread and wine as a metaphor, Jesus wanted his disciples to know that he would do anything for them, including the shredding of his body and pouring out his blood.

There were no photographers back in Jesus' time but we all have seen a very famous painting of The Last Supper by **Leonardo da Vinci.** How did he know who sat where?

↑ Event 183
Jesus predicts Peter's denial

References in the Bible
Matthew 26:34
"Truly I tell you" Jesus answered, "this very night, before the rooster crows, you will disown me three times."

Mark 14:26

Luke 22:31-34

John 13:31-38

More elaborations
The most senior and loyal disciple, Peter denied knowing Jesus, not just once but three times.

I would love to say something nasty about Peter's shameful denial, but as Jesus has taught us: *"Do not judge others."*

Event 184
Jesus convinces his disciple that he is the way to God or his Father

References in the Bible
John 14:1-30
Phillip said, "Show us the Father and that will be good enough for us."

More elaborations
Even after two years of spending time with Jesus, all disciples still did not get the message. Poor Phillip! He thought Jesus could just snap his fingers and God would appear.

Event 185
Jesus teaches about the vine and the branches

References in the Bible
John 15:1-17
My command is this: love each other as I have loved you. Greater love has no one than this: to lay down one's life for one's friends.

More elaborations
Jesus knew his twelve disciples had never gotten along well and that they would fall apart after his death.

Asking one disciple to lay down his life for the other was a tall order. That was the most important lesson from Jesus but unfortunately the Twelve did not take it to their heart.

↑ Event 186

Jesus warns about hatred in the world

References in the Bible

John 15:18-27

If you belonged to the world, it would love you as its own. As it is, you do not belong to the world, but I have chosen you out of the world. That is why the world hates you.

More elaborations

Jesus laid out the cost of following or believing in him. It was true back then and it is still true now, two thousand years later.

At the current time in 2020, there are more than 80 million of refugees around the world, especially in troubled counties (per UNHCR). It is sad to see the image of children wandering in the refugee camp. Their home is just a tiny tent made of plastic or cardboard.

If you remember from reading the **Fact II**, Jesus himself and his parents were the refugees of the First century. King Herod ordered to kill the baby Jesus. When will the hatred in the world end?

Event 187

Jesus prepares his disciples for the time of grief

References in the Bible

John 16:1-33

They will put you out of the synagogue; in fact, the time is coming when anyone who kills you will think they are offering a service to God.

So with you: now is your time of grief, but I will see you again and you will rejoice, and no one will take away your joy.

More elaborations

Only John wrote about this talk between Jesus and his disciples. Jesus tried his best to warn of the eminent danger that the disciples would face after his death.

Jesus also promised to see his disciples again in a place where they would be happy until eternity. Their life on earth would end, but the afterlife was waiting for them. Unfortunately, the disciples had not fully understood Jesus' teachings. They were all afraid of death therefore they started hiding once Jesus was arrested.

Event 188

Jesus agonizes in the Garden of Gethsemane

References in the Bible

Matthew 26:38

Then he said to them, "My soul is overwhelmed with sorrow to the point of death. Stay here and keep watch with me."

Mark 14:32

Luke 22:39

More elaborations

It's anxious time. Jesus began to question his father's plan, is this how you want me to die? Are you sure? Only Jesus knew the pending agony. His disciples had no clue.

↑ Event 189
Jesus prays for himself

References in the Bible

John 17:1-5

Father, the hour has come. Glorify your Son, that your Son may glorify you.

More elaborations

Up to this point Jesus still had time to alter his ending but perhaps the thought of "going home" was more comforting than being on Earth.

The entire Chapter 17 of John is about Jesus' prayer. Jesus knew the world was a battleground of God's authority and Satan's power. Jesus prayed that God would keep his believers away from Satan's reach.

Event 190

Jesus prays for his disciples

References in the Bible

John 17:6-19

I am coming to you now, but I say these things while I am still in this world, so that they may have the full measure of my joy with them.

My prayer is not that you take them out of the world but that you protect them from the evil one.

More elaborations

Jesus was begging God to accept his disciples as himself, son of God. Jesus asked God to protect them, especially from evil.

John recorded these prayers from Jesus for the disciples, including John himself. Perhaps during the end of Jesus' earth life, John spent more time with Jesus than any other disciples. No one else wrote about this pleading from Jesus, except John. No wonder more than a few times John referred to himself as "the disciple Jesus loved."

↑ Event 191
Jesus is betrayed and arrested

References in the Bible
Matthew 26:47-56
Now the betrayer has arranged a signal with them: "The one I kiss is the man; arrest him."

But this (Jesus' arrest) has all taken place that the writings of the prophets might be fulfilled. Then all the disciples deserted him and fled.

Mark 14:43 Luke 22:47

John 18:1-11
Then Simon Peter, who had a sword, drew it and struck the high priest' servant, cutting off his right ear. The servant's name was Malchus.

More elaborations
It must have been very painful for Jesus to see his disciples betraying and abandoning him.

Why did Peter get a sword?
Well, nowadays pastors and priests in USA are allowed to carry a gun to church so that they can protect themselves and the church attendees. Not sure if this is an evidence of lacking faith in God or Jesus. Or these ministers may think to themselves that God is too far away and too busy to protect them?

Event 192

Jesus answers to Annas (father-in-law of Caiaphas, the high priest)

References in the Bible

John 18:12-24

I always taught in synagogues or at the temple, where all the Jews come together. I said nothing in secret. Why question me?

When Jesus said this, one of the officials nearby slapped him in the face.

More elaborations

The high priests and their religious gang wanted to insult Jesus any way they could. Humanity was at its worst.

This event happened almost two thousand years ago, but somehow I can visualize it clearly like I was there. What a painful experience for our poor Jesus!

Event 193
Caiaphas (Chief Priest/son-in-law of Annas) questions Jesus

References in the Bible

Matthew 26:57-68

Then they spat on his (Jesus) face and struck him with their fists. Others slapped him and said, "Prophesy to us, Messiah. Who hits you?"

Mark 14:53

More elaborations

How could the religious leaders treat Jesus worse than a human being? These God-loving fanatics were so evil. Unfortunately some of the religious leaders of modern time are still behaving the same way.

With so much power in their hands they feel they can get away with the crime of abusing young victims or stealing money from the church. And with the same power they can punish whoever reports their crime.

↑ Event 194

As predicted, Peter denied knowing Jesus

References in the Bible

Matthew 26:69-75

Then he (Peter) began to call down curses, and he swore to them, "I don't know the man (Jesus)."

Mark 14:66

Luke 22:54

John 18:25-27

More elaborations

Not sure why Peter was chosen as the gatekeeper of heaven? Was it a punishment? I could see how busy the job would be. Besides, no one would ever come back to thank the gatekeeper once they were already inside.

Event 195
Jesus was turned over to the Roman Governor named Pilate

References in the Bible
Matthew 27:1-2
So they bound him (Jesus), led him away and handed him over to Pilate the Governor.

Mark 15:1

Luke 22:66

More elaborations
The Jewish religious leaders did not have the authority to kill Jesus. They needed the Roman Governor to do the dirty job.

Event 196
Judas paid the price

References in the Bible

Matthew 27:3-7

So Judas threw the money into the temple and left. Then he went away and hanged himself.

The chief priest picked up the coins and said, "It is against the law to put this into the treasury since it is blood money." So they decided to use the money to buy the potter's field as a burial place for foreigners.

More elaborations

Perhaps returning the money was Judas' best action of his entire life. And as a result of his betrayal, the foreigners ended up with a burial place for themselves in Israel.

Event 197
Jesus stands trial before Pilate

References in the Bible

Matthew 27:11-14

Meanwhile Jesus stood before the governor, and the governor asked him, "Are you the king of the Jews?"

Mark 15:2-5 Luke 23:1-5

John 18:28-38

You (Roman Governor Pilate) say that I am the king. In fact the reason I was born and came into the world is to testify to the truth. Everyone on the side of the truth listens to me.

More elaborations

Very sure Governor Pilate had no idea what Jesus was talking about. Governor Pilate thought the word "King" was the real king who had authority over the Jews or at least a tribe of many people.

All Roman soldiers made fun of Jesus when they realized he was just a king of the imaginary world (afterlife). But for once, the two worlds collided. The most damaged one turned out to be our real world.

↑ Event 198
Jesus stands trial before King Herod

References in the Bible

Luke 23:6-10

When Herod saw Jesus, he was greatly pleased, because for a long time he had been wanting to see him.

More elaborations

Jesus had a chance to avoid death but chose to ignore the opportunity. Also it would have been an insult to the spirit of John the Baptist if Jesus received any favor from the one who killed him.

This incidence can be understood as an ultimate temptation for Jesus. We all want to live longer even just for a few extra seconds. That was not the case with Jesus. He did not want to accept this offer or succumb to this temptation.

↑Event 199

Roman Governor Pilate wants to pardon Jesus

References in the Bible

John 19:8-10

Don't you realize I have power either to free you or to crucify you?

More elaborations

Jesus had already set out to die for mankind. He was not interested in making deals. Still, if Jesus had any compassion left for his disciples and his followers he might have wanted to hang onto his earthy life for a little while longer.

Actually, there are a lot of discussions about this event. What would Jesus do with the extra time? Could he fix the rift among his disciples? Could Jesus make all disciples as caring as he was? Would Jesus pick a replacement for him?

One thing is for sure: if Jesus did not die and lived to his old age then all we would have is a religion built around his teachings. He would be honored along with other greats like John the Baptist, Buddha and Confucius.

Event 200
Pilate hands Jesus over to be crucified

References in the Bible
Matthew 27:15-26
Which of the two (Jesus Barabbas and Jesus the Messiah) do you want me to release to you? "Barabbas", they answered.

Mark 15:6-15

Luke 23:13-25

John 18:39 & 19:16

More elaborations
Interesting coincidence! There were two prisoners both named Jesus. The governor could pardon one but the Jewish religious leaders chose to save Jesus the thief instead!

Event 201
Roman soldiers made fun of Jesus

References in the Bible
Matthew 27:27-30
They spat on him (Jesus), and took the staff and struck him on the head again and again.

Mark 15:16-20

Luke 23:11

More elaborations
Not sure where the real hell is, but on that day and at that place, Jesus must have been in hell.

Over the course of our lifetime sooner or later we will face hell ourselves. Think about it!

↓ Event 202

Jesus is led away to be crucified

References in the Bible

Matthew 27:32-44

As they (soldiers and prisoners) were going out, they met a man from Cyrene, named Simon, and they (soldiers) forced him to carry the cross (for Jesus).

Mark 15:21-24

Luke 23:26-31

John 19:17-18

More elaborations

Simon of Cyrene was the last person on earth to do a good thing for Jesus!

Perhaps the main message Jesus left is how cruel humans can be. Although nothing like the violence and cruelty that happened in the Old Testament, seeing someone being nailed on the cross is very graphic by any standard. Jesus' painful death dragged on slowly.

↑ Event 203
Pilate puts a sign on the cross

References in the Bible
<u>John 19:19-22</u>
Pilate had a notice prepared and fastened to the cross. It read: "Jesus of Nazareth, the King of the Jews."

More elaborations
Regardless who Jesus actually was, having him crucified by the foreigner group (Romans) was an insult to Jesus and his followers. Still, the ugliness of betrayal by his disciple and his own people was the darkest event in Jewish history.

↑ Event 204

Jesus' last words to his mother, Mary, and "the disciple whom he loved"

References in the Bible

John 19:25-27

He said to her (Mary), "Woman, here is your son," and to the disciple, "Here is your mother." From that time on, this disciple (John) took her into his home."

More elaborations

According to John, he was Jesus' favorite or the most beloved disciple. Therefore, there was no surprise when Jesus asked John to take care of his mother. John happily obliged and brought Mary home to his house.

↑Event 205
Jesus' last follower
(a thief named Dimas; the name was given by Bible scholars later and might not be his real name)

References in the Bible
Luke 23:40-43
Then he said, "Jesus, remember me when you come into your kingdom."

Jesus answered him, "Truly I tell you today you will be with me in paradise."

More elaborations
While he was being crucified on the cross, Jesus redeemed a criminal who believed in him.

The dying criminal (named Dimas) had more faith in Jesus than most of Jesus' followers, including the twelve disciples.

Event 206
Jesus' last drink

References in the Bible
John 19:28-29
Jesus said, "I am thirsty." A jar of wine vinegar was there, so they soaked a sponge in it, put the sponge on a stalk of the hyssop plant, and lifted it to Jesus' lips.

More elaborations
Only John wrote about Jesus saying that he was thirsty. The name of whoever gave Jesus his last drink was not recorded. Just wonder, who was that person, a Roman soldier?

↔ Event 207
Jesus' last words, before dying on the cross

References in the Bible
Matthew 27:46
*About three in the afternoon Jesus cried out in a loud voice, "**Eli, Eli, lema sabachthani?**" (which means "My God, my God, why have you forsaken me?)"*

Mark 15:33

Luke 23:44-46
Father, into your hands I commit my spirit.

John 19:30
It is finished.

More elaborations
Matthew and Mark had the same Jesus' last words. Luke and John wrote something else. That is understandable since none of them was with Jesus at his death. They wrote down according to the accounts or stories of others who were with Jesus when he died.

Jesus' last words were not as important as his last image: a very thin, bleeding body hanging on the cross. How agonizing!

↓ Event 208

Jesus dies on the cross at the age of 35 or 36

References in the Bible

Matthew 27:50

And when Jesus had cried out again in a loud voice, he gave up his spirit.

Mark 15:37

With a loud cry, Jesus breathed his last.

Luke 23:44   John 19:30

More elaborations

What a painful death! The physical torture of the body being pulled down by gravity while the hands and feet are nailed to the cross must be incredible. The shear-stress applies to the flesh would make anyone, human or God, scream out loudly until death.

No indication what Jesus said at the second time! However, for almost two thousand years people have not stopped talking about Jesus' state of mind at the last minute. They think Jesus was in pain according to Matthew and Mark. Meanwhile by reading gospels of Luke and John, they think Jesus was calm and looked forward to seeing his Father in heaven. It is a slight contradiction for you and me to figure out.

↔ Event 209

Four major violent events happened during Jesus' death

References in the Bible

Matthew 27:51

At that moment the curtain of the temple was torn in two from top to bottom. The earth shook, the rocks split and the tomb broke open.

More elaborations

A major earthquake could have caused all the violence and damages described by Matthew. Still, it is hard to deny the link between this coincidence and the horrific death of Jesus.

While people were celebrating Easter Sunday on April 12, 2020 in the USA, several big tornadoes ripped through many states and killed over 40 people. The country has already lost over 20,000 lives because of the COVID-19 pandemic. Why the tornadoes? People already suffered enough because of the virus. Perhaps it is a message from God but we don't know for sure.

↔ Event 210

The resurrection of other holy people

References in the Bible

<u>Matthew 27:52-53</u>

They came out of the tombs after Jesus' resurrection and went into the holy city and appeared to many people.

<u>Matthew 27:57-61</u>

Joseph took the body (of Jesus), wrapped it in a clean linen cloth, and placed it in his own new tomb that he has cut out of the rock.

More elaborations

Just wonder about the identities of the "holy people", who were also raised to life right after Jesus' death?

Matthew appears to have this event out of sequence. He used the phrase "Jesus' resurrection" before mentioning about Joseph's burial plan for Jesus, see **Event 212**.

Event 211
The women who were with Jesus at his death

References in the Bible

Matthew 27:55

Many women were there, watching from a distance. They had followed Jesus from Galilee to care for his needs. Among them were Mary Magdalene, Mary the mother of James and Joseph (Jesus' aunt), and the mother of Zebedee's sons.

Mark 15:40 John 19:25-26

More elaborations

Jesus' ministry or the entourage of 13 people (minimum) was a big burden to any budget keeper. Plus Judas himself was a crook so financing Jesus' ministry was a huge task.

The expenses for clothing, food, lodging, and teaching would have been very high. These devoted women were the main financiers since Jesus and these 12 disciples did not have paying jobs.

Meanwhile the remaining 11 disciples were in hiding!

Event 212

Jesus is laid in the tomb by Joseph, a member of the Council, with the help from Nicodemus

References in the Bible

Matthew 27:57-59

Joseph took the body (of Jesus) and placed it in his own new tomb that he had cut out of the rock. He rolled a big stone in front of the entrance to the tomb and went away.

Mark 15:42

Luke 23:50-56

John 19:38

More elaborations

To avoid prosecution by the Romans, all the remaining 11 disciples of Jesus had disappeared. Joseph of Arimathea took their place in burying Jesus' body.

Event 213

Guards are posted at Jesus' tomb

References in the Bible

Matthew 27:62-65

"Take a guard," Pilate answered. "Go make the tomb as secure as you know how." So they went and made the tomb secure by putting a seal on the stone and posting the guard.

More elaborations

Since Jesus had told everyone that he would rise up from the dead, Pilate wanted to make sure Jesus' disciples could not break into the tomb and steal Jesus' body.

↔ Event 214
Jesus' resurrection

References in the Bible

Matthew 28:1-7

He has risen from the dead and is going ahead of you into Galilee. There you will see him.

Mark 16:1-8

Luke 24:1-12

In their fright the women bowed down with their faces to the ground, but the men (angels) said to them, "Why do you look for the living among the dead?"

John 20:1-10

More elaborations

An angel of God appeared to Mary Magdalene and Mary (Jesus' aunt). He told them Jesus has come back as he promised.

Matthew recorded that only one angel appeared to the women while Luke mentioned two angels.

↑ Event 215
Jesus first appears to Mary Magdalene

References in the Bible

Matthew 28:8-10

Suddenly Jesus met them. "Greetings", he said. They came to him, clasped his feet and worshipped him.

Mark 16:9-11

She went and told those who had been with him and who were mourning and weeping.

John 20:11-18

More elaborations

Mark and John wrote that Jesus first appeared to Mary Magdalene only. Why her?

Perhaps it's because she had been very devoted and faithful to Jesus and his ministry, unlike the twelve disciples. One betrayed Jesus and the rest abandoned him when he was in trouble.

Event 216

Jesus appears to two believers on the road

References in the Bible

Mark 16:12-13

Afterward Jesus appeared in a different form to two of them while they were walking in the country. These returned and reported it to the rest; but they (disciples and public) did not believe them (two believers) either.

Luke 24:13-35

More elaborations

Of all the stories of Jesus' resurrection, that was the one when Jesus spent the longest time after his death. He even went home and had dinner with them. At first they thought of Jesus as a stranger on the road but then recognized him when he broke and shared bread with them.

↑ Event 217

Jesus appears to his disciples including Thomas (who was not convinced that Jesus had risen from the dead)

References in the Bible

Mark 16:14

Later Jesus appeared to the Eleven as they were eating; he rebuked them for their lack of faith and their stubborn refusal to believe those who had seen him after he had risen.

Luke 24:36-43

Touch me and see; a ghost does not have flesh and bones, as you see I have.

Luke 24:41-42

They gave him a piece of broiled fish, and he took it and ate it in their presence.

John 20:24-31

More elaborations

Why did Jesus bother to see these 11 unfaithful disciples again? Like a good parent, Jesus just could not give them up completely. Perhaps they would turn out OK once they grew up! Per Luke 24:36-43, that was the first evidence of Jesus "believing" in ghosts.

Event 218

Religious leaders bribe the guards to keep their mouth shut

References in the Bible

Matthew 28:11-15

So the soldiers took the money and did as they were instructed. And this story has been widely circulated among the Jews to this very day.

More elaborations

The world would be a better place without these religious leaders. Their lies were used to kill Jesus and their lies were also used to hide Jesus' resurrection.

Event 219

Jesus appears and has his last meal with the seven disciples

References in the Bible

John 21:1-14

Jesus came, took the bread and gave it to them, and did the same with the fish.

More elaborations

Before leaving earth, Jesus wanted to have one more round of good times with his disciples. Again, only John wrote about this significant event, not Matthew.

According to the Old Testament (Book of Genesis) God always likes grilled or BBQ lamb and beef. Unlike his Father, Jesus often was mentioned eating fish and bread. You may say in the case of Jesus "*the apple does fall far away from its tree*".

↑ Event 220
Jesus' last lesson for his disciple Peter, and for all of us

References in the Bible
John 21:15-18
Very truly I tell you, when you were younger you dressed yourself and went where you wanted; but when you are old you will stretch out your hands, and someone else will dress you and lead you where you do NOT want to go.

More elaborations
That is very true for many leaders, including the Pope. He would rather dress himself casually and walk to a public park or a local pub than perform the duties that the Vatican wanted him to do.

Event 221
The rumor of John the disciple to be immortal

References in the Bible
John 21:20-23
If I want him (John, the disciple whom Jesus loved) to remain alive until I return, what is that to you?

More elaborations
John for sure wanted the readers to know he was the teacher's favorite student. You be the judge!

John deserves the credit for taking care of Mary, Jesus' mother, after the death of Jesus.

Event 222

Jesus gives the great commission

References in the Bible

Matthew 28:16

Therefore go and make disciples of all nations, baptizing them in the name of the Father and the Son and the Holy Spirit.

Mark 16:15

More elaborations

Jesus' last teaching appeared to be working. Although most of the work was done by Paul, more than any disciple of Jesus (read more about Paul in the book of ACTS).

↕ Event 223
Jesus ascends into heaven

References in the Bible

Mark 16:19

After the Lord Jesus had spoken to them, he was taken into heaven and he sat at the right hand of God.

Luke 24:50-53

More elaborations

No details of how Jesus "was taken into heaven". Also, who told Mark and Luke about Jesus getting a seat next to God?

By now I hope you realize that Jesus is a holy spirit, like God. He does not have a lazy physical body that needs to be seated like the rest of us.

Question for readers

Q1: What is the same between Heaven and Hell?

A: *We try to avoid both places at all cost!*

And final question: Where do you keep your GOD Folder or GOD File?

Why not? You had files for everything else from A to Z.

Final Few Words from the Author

I started to work on this book right after I was discharged from hospital, sometimes in August of 2019. For over 10 months I had been treated by the two biggest hospitals in Brisbane (Queensland, Australia) for my Leukemia disease. Since I was over 63 years old with a couple of underlining illnesses, the chance of me surviving this cancer was almost zero. In fact, on November 2, 2018, while sitting in my hospital room, my wife heard a thumping sound from the toilet. I had passed out and fell to the floor. She screamed out for help then a team of nurses and doctors rushed in to revive me. I had already lost all my vital signs. Without her being in the room it would have been too late for the medical team to bring me back to life.

Knowing that I had survived poverty, childhood malaria disease, brutal war, and the boat journey to freedom, Mr. Rex Ward, my first English teacher (see his reference below) compared me to a cat with nine lives. He was very sure that I still had one or two lives left and would overcome my leukemia illness. Since he was right, I decided to write this booklet in honor of him, and the people who believe in miracles. All my near death experiences cannot be a result of pure coincidence or pure luck. I am the witness of God's miraculous work and this book is the testimony.

Perhaps the one who suffered more than me during my cancer treatment was my wife. Every day she came to the hospital early in the morning with new supplies and my favorite food. At evening time she went home alone, sad and worried. She knew my chance of survival was very slim, but still she had strong faith in God, Jesus, and especially the Virgin Mary. Since 1999 she has received many miracles from the Virgin Mary, she believed. Without any doubt, she knew the Virgin Mary would not fail her this time. She begged the Virgin Mary, Jesus, and God to save me.

The New Testament only referred to Jesus' mother a few times and nothing was mentioned about her Holiness or sacredness. But to most Catholic followers she is even more sacred than Jesus. Every Catholic Church has a statue of the Virgin Mary and many church services that are devoted to her. I love and respect my wife so whatever makes her feel safe and blessed is a good part of my life as well. Nothing wrong with believing and worshipping the mother of Jesus, especially the mother who raised a caring and courageous son!

The timing of this book could not be better. The world is fighting the Covid-19 pandemic. Most people are staying home either voluntarily or by force from the government. All priorities in life are finally corrected by this unfortunate event. Nurses, doctors, medical researchers, medical staff, farmers, food supply workers, and delivery folk are correctly respected and recognized as the important part of our daily life. Football heroes, sports figures, and entertainment celebrities are taking a back seat. No more long lines to the stadiums or theatres. Instead, people are forming long lines at dawn in front of the supermarkets, trying to purchase the essentials like water, salt, sugar, flour, meat, and toilet paper.

Hopefully this book will help you to find God sooner, if you have not found our Divine yet. Unlike my case, I wish you don't have to endure a hell-like torture before you look for Jesus or God. It will be a much more pleasant conversation with God when you are healthy or not in pain. But like most of us, we don't think about God when we are cruising smoothly on the highway heading to our beach front resort.

These days it might seem more difficult to feel connected to God but in fact it's quite the opposite. Many of us usually tend to be near a phone or tablet, and though these devices can be distractions, they can also be used to access the word of God and find your comfort zone again at any time. With it, I hope that you also keep an electronic copy of my book, a guardrail to protect you from falling off your path. May your life journey be forever in peace, my best regard!

My sincere thanks to the Angels who have saved my life

- My brother "Seventh" (Anh Bảy) for jumping into the river and saving me from drowning. He was 10 years old and I was 4 years old (in 1959).
- **UNICEF** for saving me from dying from malaria. I was 13 years old (in 1968). They also provided me with a scholarship for college. Please watch: https://www.facebook.com/UNICEF-USA/videos/10154771405190797/
- American and South Vietnamese soldiers for holding their fire during a crossfire that allowed me to cross a bridge safely. The enemy soldiers still kept shooting but missed me.
- An unknown spirit in an unestablished cemetery that told me and my friend to return home instead of trying to escape by foot into Thailand from Pleiku Province, Central Vietnam, in 1976. We would be shot if we kept going further west.
- The Taiwanese Captain of two fishing ships, named **Jin-An Song (宋謹安):** he saved me and 28 other boat people from drowning in South China Sea (on July 9th 1978). You can read more of this miracle and how I found him after 40 years: https://humanityatitsbest.org/
- **Pete Bannister** of Stillwater, Minnesota USA: my leg was caught in an industrial mixer. Without

Peter I would be dead due to excessive bleeding. We were the only two left in the building.

- **Princess Alexandra Hospital,** Brisbane, Queensland, Australia, and **Dr. Robert Bird**, **Dr. Peter Wood**, along with great nurses, and support staff.
- **Royal Brisbane and Women's Hospital,** Brisbane, Queensland, Australia, where my bone-marrow transplant took place. My chance of survival was slim but **Dr. Siok Tey** and the staff of **Cancer Care Services** saved me.
- The unknown 37-years-old American man who donated his healthy bone marrow to me.
- Members of **Vietnam Grace Church Brisbane** and several non-Christian friends from around the world who have prayed for me to have a successful bone marrow transplant.
- My wife, Diamond, who discovered me unconscious on Nov 2, 2018. Without her screaming out for help I would have died.
- Our children **Timothy** (wife Kristel, daughter Rebecca, and son Isaac), **Andrew**, and **Jessica** for their love and full support.
- Just for our daughter Jessica alone, thank you for giving me the **Holy Bible** (New International Version) that I could read and understand.
- And finally, thank you, **God** for opening my eyes and "choosing" me as your messenger. Our world is in a chaotic situation. It has too many problems that I don't think any human being on

Earth can solve. Not sure if I can fix anything but I will try my best to spread your message of love and forgiveness.

-

I also want to thank those who have made my life better:

- The 1st **Australian Civil Affair Unit** and **Mr. Rex Ward** who first taught me English 52 years ago. Our reunion story was written and published online by **Griffith University**: https://griffithreview.com/articles/fifty-years-five-hundred-miles-play-voices/
- The **Country of Indonesia** for accepting me, along with thousands of other refugees from Vietnam during the late 1970s.
- Pastor **George Stormont** from the UK whom I met on the plane from Minneapolis to Duluth Minnesota USA on Feb 09, 1979. Besides helping me to get from the frozen tarmac into the terminal safely he also gave me a small plaque card with the **Footprints in the Sand** story.
- The **Boyd (Robert & Charlotte)**, **Milbrath (Cy & Mary), Miller (Ray & Phyllis)** and **Dahl (Arthur and Carol)** families in Duluth, MN USA. These four families sponsored me, as a new arrival from the refugee camp in Indonesia.
- **University of Minnesota**
- **Vietnam Veterans of America**

- **Vietnam Veterans Associations of Australia, Sunshine Coast Sub-Branch**
- **John and Eileen Cunnington;** John is a Vietnam Veteran and a writer. Both he and his wife, Eileen, helped me to complete this booklet.
- **Wallaby Airlines, 35 Squadron Royal Australian Air Force**
- **Queensland Health Department** for completely covering my Leukemia treatments without taking a penny from my pocket.
- **Pastor Vince Barringer** and **Good Shepherd Lutheran Church** in Downey, California USA where I was baptized on March 16, 2020.
- **Mr. Gary Knox of PRC-DeSoto International** (a division of **PPG Industries),** who first hired me as a young engineer without any experience.
- **Strong & Bold Publishing**, Adelaide, SA Australia

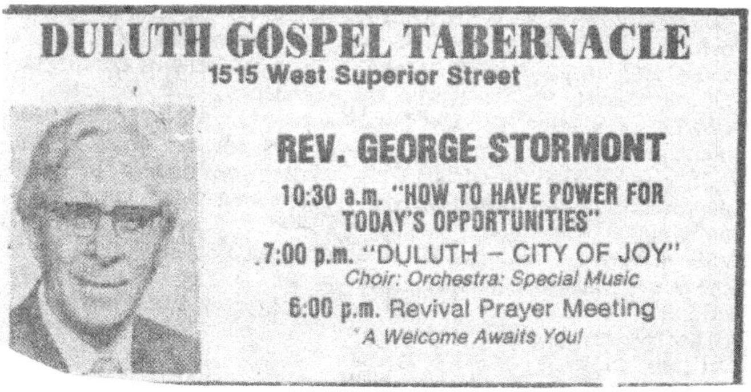

Did God send this angel to help me on Feb 09, 1979?

THANK YOU

INDEX of Jesus' Teaching

<u>Note:</u> Jesus' teaching does not cover everything that we are dealing with in modern time. But we can use his basic guideline to solve our issues or enrich our life. Also please note that one Event may have more than one merits so it would appear under two or more places.

<u>Relating to the wellbeing or feeling:</u>

<u>About Life Enhancements</u>:

YOUR NOTES: